The Incredible
SCIENCE PUZZLE
CHALLENGE

HELENE HOVANEC

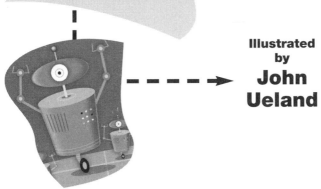

Illustrated
by
**John
Ueland**

Sterling Publishing Co., Inc.
New York

Contents

10 9 8 7 6 5 4 3 2 1

Published by Sterling Publishing Co., Inc.
387 Park Avenue South, New York, NY 10016
© 2003, 2000 by Helene Hovanec
Distributed in Canada by Sterling Publishing
C/o Canadian Manda Group, One Atlantic Avenue, Suite 105
Toronto, Ontario, Canada M6K 3E7
Distributed in Great Britain by Chrysalis Books
64 Brewery Road, London N7 9NT, England
Distributed in Australia by Capricorn Link (Australia) Pty. Ltd.
P.O. Box 704, Windsor, NSW 2756, Australia

Manufactured in the United States of America
All rights reserved

Sterling ISBN 1-4027-0716-9

Introduction

Welcome to Firefly Labs, where mad scientist Dr. Duncan Dunkendorf and I work tirelessly to save the future!

You're probably wondering why we've summoned you here. Well, we have an urgent problem and desperately need your help. Dr. Dunkendorf and I have just discovered that our nemesis, the evil Dr. Frick, is only hours away from unleashing a massive amount of deadly robots—these malevolent machines are part of Dr. Frick's plot to take over the world, and are set to destroy everything in their path!

But all may not be lost. Our latest creation, the Zagbar-5000, is able to send a signal that will change the settings on these robots from "Destroy" to "Dance!" The only problem is the Zagbar-5000 won't work without the password, and Dr. Dunkendorf, genius scientist that he is, can't remember it!

Only by completing the puzzles in this book can you uncover the password. There's no time to waste, but we will be there with you along the way. And don't worry, we know you can save us—and the whole world!

— 1 —

Dunkendorf's Mad Mindbenders

No wonder Albert Einstein had crazy white hair and a kooky look in his eye. Scientific words and phrases are enough to make even geniuses cry, "No more hypotheses!"

But you can dive into the basics by completing the puzzles in this section. Here you'll explore some basic vocabulary, learn about famous scientists, and discover what deer meat and snake poison have in common. Oh! And you'll also help us get closer to the secret password...

Science Study

For your first test, figure out the answer to the clue in the parentheses ( ). Write that word in the empty spaces on each line to find the field of science that studies the subject given in the brackets [ ].

1. (piece of wood)   B I O __ __ __ Y

   [living things]

2. (device for catching fish)

   E L E C T R O M A G __ __ __ I S M

   [electricity]

3. (sob)   __ __ __ O G E N I C S

   [the effects of very low temperatures]

4. (conclusion)   D __ __ __ R O L O G Y

   [trees and woody plants]

5. (small rug)   C L I __ __ __ O L O G Y

   [climates]

6. (cab)   __ __ __ __ D E R M Y

   [stuffing and mounting animals]

7. (not short)   M E __ __ __ __ U R G Y

   [metals]

8. (curved doorway feature)

    __ __ __ __ A E O L O G Y [past cultures]

9. (steal from) __ __ __ O T I C S

[self-controlled machines]

10. (a ballplayer for Houston)

    __ __ __ __ __ N O M Y

[matter in outer space]

11. (your dog or cat, for example)

    H E R __ __ __ O L O G Y

[reptiles and amphibians]

12. (short for Thomas) A N A __ __ __ Y

[body structure of plants and animals]

13. (light brown) B O __ __ __ Y [plants]

14. (ran into) __ __ __ E O R O L O G Y

[weather]

15. (animal park) __ __ __ L O G Y [animals]

Answer on page 120.

The Machine Age

Write a letter in the blank space on each line to spell the name of a machine. Then read down the starred column to find the name of the science that deals with machines and the way people use them.

*

JACKHAMM __ R

HA __ VESTER

__ ENERATOR

BULLD __ ZER

TURBI __ E

C __ PIER

CO __ PRESSOR

TYPEWR __ TER

__ OMPUTER

FAC __ IMILE

Answer on page 117.

Habitats for Scientists

All living things need a habitat, or special place, of their own. Some of the habitats studied by scientists are scattered below. Put them in alphabetical order into the grid and then read down the *starred* column. You'll find the first and last names of a famous marine biologist and writer.

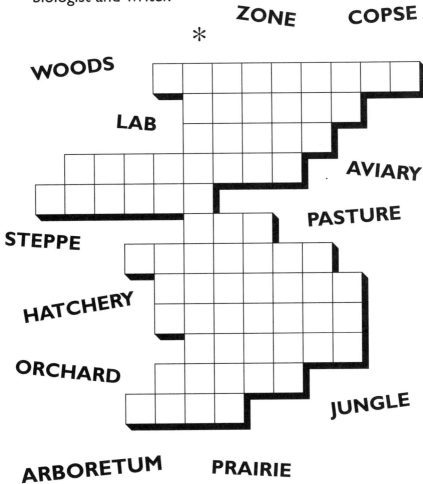

ZONE   COPSE

WOODS

LAB

AVIARY

PASTURE

STEPPE

HATCHERY

ORCHARD

JUNGLE

ARBORETUM   PRAIRIE

Answer on page 121.

Three Close Relatives

Change one letter in each word to find three words that belong together in each group. Write the new words on the lines. The first one is done for you.

1. **Dogs**

   FIX MERRIER   <u>FOX TERRIER</u>

   TREAT LANE   _____

   DRENCH NOODLE   _____

2. **Insects**

   MELLOW PACKET   _____

   COACH   _____

   WAFER MUG   _____

3. **Fish**

   CROOK GROUT   _____

   SLING ROY   _____

   BLOCK TEA LASS   _____

4. **Amphibians**

   FLOG   _____

   GOAD   _____

   NEWS   _____

5. **Mammals**

   MILD BOAT   _____

   MOLAR HEAR   _____

   GLUE BOX   _____

6. Forest Workers

MARK DANGER _____

JOGGER _____

GOOD SHOPPER _____

7. Plant Parts

STEW _____

LEAD _____

BOOT _____

8. Birds

LOVE _____

GAWK _____

CARROT _____

9. Precipitation

FLEET _____

SHOW _____

WAIL _____

10. Metals

BOLD _____

SOLVER _____

HOPPER _____

11. Snakes

ODDER _____

WIPER _____

TATTLER _____

Answer on page 122.

Center Line

Put one letter into each blank space below to spell a common 7-letter word. Then, read down the starred column to answer this riddle:

What kind of jokes did Einstein make?

*

ANS__ERS

SHR__VEL

BLI__TER

PAL__TTE

KNU__KLE

IMP__OVE

FAN__TIC

TEA__HER

MAN__IND

PEA__ANT

Now do the same thing with these words to answer another riddle:

What snack food do geologists like?

*

EME__ALD

DEP__SIT

WEL__OME

BOO__LET

HAT__HET

ADV__NCE

GRA__ITE

SAN__BAR

COP__CAT

Answer on page 121.

A to Z

Scientists are curious people, which makes them do certain things. What do they do? Select one letter from the alphabet below and put it into each blank space to make words that describe what scientists often do as they work. Cross off each letter after using it, because it will only be used once.

A B C D E F G H I J K L M N

O P Q R S T U V W X Y Z

E__ AMINE

__ UERY

__ EMAND

DISCO__ ER

INVESTI__ ATE

SEARC__

SEE__

Q__ IZ

INS__ ECT

TR__

SA__ PLE

RECOGNI__ E

__ TUDY

__ SK

O__ SERVE

S__ RUTINIZE

EXP__ AIN

__ NQUIRE

DE__ ERMINE

PR__ BE

__ UDGE

__ IGURE OUT

P__ OVE

V__ RIFY

U__ EARTH

REVIE__

Answer on page 116.

Scientific Research #1

The name of each scientist in the righthand column contains a word that fits the numbered clue. To find this word, cross off some letters in the scientist's name, and then read the remaining letters from left to right.

Example: Money _CASH_ CA~~VEND~~I~~S~~H

Clue/Answer	**Scientist**
1. Type of bed	
_____	BURBANK
2. Fishing rod	
_____	PTOLEMY
3. Bear's home	
_____	CARVER
4. Crusted dessert	
_____	OPPENHEIMER
5. Female deer	
_____	DOOLEY
6. Cooling device	
_____	FEYNMAN

7. Strong wind

_____   GALILEO

8. Type of phone

_____   MITCHELL

9. Heal

_____   CURIE

10. Relax

_____   PRIESTLEY

11. Spoil

_____   ROENTGEN

12. Baby farm animal

_____   CHADWICK

13. Lock opener

_____   KENNY

14. Map

_____   CHARCOT

15. School vehicle

_____   BUNSEN

Answer on page 125.

A Doctor in the House?

A two-letter word was removed from each health care worker in the list below and placed in the box. Put each missing piece in the correct blanks to name the worker whose specialty is described in the parentheses ( ) below.

AD	AN	AT	EN	ER
HI	HO	IS	IT	MA
ME	ON	OP	OR	OX

1. P E D I ___ ___ R I C I A N

   (doctor who takes care of babies and children)

2. ___ ___ T H O P E D I S T

   (doctor who specializes in skeletal problems)

3. D E R ___ ___ T O L O G I S T

   (doctor who deals with skin problems)

4. P S Y C ___ ___ A T R I S T

   (doctor who specializes in mental disorders)

5. O B S T E T R I C I ___ ___

   (doctor who delivers babies)

6. N E U R O L O G __ __ T
(nervous system doctor)

7. P A R A __ __ D I C
(person who helps doctors give emergency treatment)

8. N U T R __ __ I O N I S T
(food specialist)

9. S U R G E __ __
(doctor who performs operations)

10. C H I R __ __ O D I S T
(foot specialist)

11. D __ __ T I S T
(doctor who takes care of teeth)

12. O R T __ __ D O N T I S T
(doctor who straightens teeth)

13. R __ __ I O L O G I S T
(x-ray specialist)

14. T __ __ I C O L O G I S T
(poison specialist)

15. T H __ __ A P I S T
(person who helps patients recover their physical abilities)

Answer on page 121.

Same Starts

Each group of scientific words starts with the same three letters (which may or may not be a real word). Use the clues in the parentheses ( ) to help you decide which letters to place in the blanks.

1. __ __ __ O M (snake's poison)
   __ __ __ U S (second planet from the sun)
   __ __ __ I S O N (deer meat)

2. __ __ __ A S S I U M (silver-white metal used in making fertilizer)
   __ __ __ A T O (underground vegetable)
   __ __ __ E N T (strong, like a vaccine)

3. __ __ __ A B O L I S M (activities that living things do to stay alive)
   __ __ __ R I C (type of measurement system)
   __ __ __ H O D (scientific procedure)

4. __ __ __ C E R (harmful disease)
   __ __ __ N I B A L (person who eats human flesh)
   __ __ __ Y O N (deep valley with high sides)

5. __ __ __ L B L A D D E R (organ near the liver)
   __ __ __ L O N (liquid measurement)
   __ __ __ A P A G O S (islands where many endangered species live)

6. __ __ __ C I U M (essential for strong teeth)

__ __ __ O R I E S (units to measure heat)

__ __ __ L U S (hard spot on the skin)

7. __ __ __ O N (wading bird)

__ __ __ R I N G (small fish)

__ __ __ E D I T Y (process of passing traits from parent to child)

8. __ __ __ R E S T (world's highest mountain)

__ __ __ R G L A D E S (swampy area in Florida)

__ __ __ R G R E E N (type of tree)

9. __ __ __ R I F I E D (stonelike wood)

__ __ __ R O L E U M (material used for making fuel)

__ __ __ R I D I S H (used to study bacteria)

10. __ __ __ A L T (metallic element used in alloys)

__ __ __ W E B (spider's product)

__ __ __ R A (poisonous snake)

11. __ __ __ M P A N Z E E (ape)

__ __ __ P M U N K (squirrel-like animal)

__ __ __ C K E N P O X (childhood disease)

12. __ __ __ R F I S H (sea animal with five arms)

__ __ __ R C H (what rice and potatoes contain)

__ __ __ M I N A (endurance)

Answer on page 118.

Mini Fill-Ins #1

Complete each grid by putting the words into the spaces where they belong.

Elements

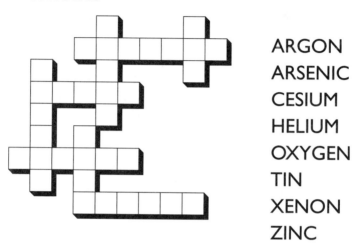

ARGON
ARSENIC
CESIUM
HELIUM
OXYGEN
TIN
XENON
ZINC

Water Places

AQUEDUCT
CANAL
FJORD
INLET
RESERVOIR
STRAIT
TRENCH

National Parks

ACADIA
ARCHES
HALEAKALA
OLYMPIC
YELLOWSTONE
YOSEMITE
ZION

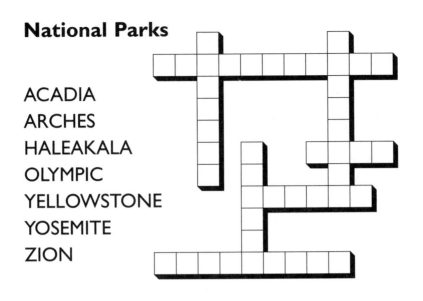

Dangerous Sea Critters

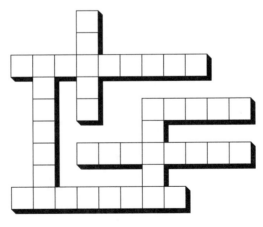

ANEMONE   MORAY EEL   SHARK
BARRACUDA   SEA SNAKE   SQUID
CORAL

Answer on page 127.

Four Close Relatives

Change one letter in each word to find four words that belong together in each group. Write the new words on the lines. The first one is done for you.

1. Face Parts

SAW   J A W

SOUTH   _____

CREEK   _____

SIPS   _____

2. Flowers

DAIRY   _____

NOSE   _____

SWEEP TEA   _____

LILT ON THY GALLEY   _____

3. Trees

SEEPING PILLOW   _____

LATE BALM   _____

SHERRY   _____

MINE   _____

4. Fruits

DRAPE   _____

SLUM   _____

TEACH   _____

AMPLE   _____

5. Leg Parts

ANGLE _____

KNEW _____

FORT _____

THIN _____

6. Arm Parts

WHIST _____

HANK _____

LINGER _____

BUNNY ZONE _____

7. Meats

PARK _____

STEAM _____

DEAL _____

LAME _____

8. Vegetables

SEAS _____

LAMA JEANS _____

STRONG DEANS _____

SQUISH _____

8. Body Organs

RIVER _____

RUNGS _____

HEARD _____

DRAIN _____

Answer on page 118.

General Science

Some terms used by scientists are in the list below. To find them, figure out the answer to the clue in the parentheses ( ) on the left. Then write that word in the empty spaces on each line to find the word that answers the clue in the brackets [ ] on the right.

1. (cult) I N __ __ __ __ I C I D E
[poisonous spray used on plants]

2. (ripped) __ __ __ __ A D O [twister]

3. (get into picture position)
D E C O M __ __ __ __
[break down into small pieces]

4. (bee's home) S __ __ __ __ R I N G
[the body's reaction to cold]

5. (what you wear over pajamas)
M I C __ __ __ __ S [tiny living creatures]

6. (handle a difficult situation)
M I C R O S __ __ __ __ [lensed instrument]

7. (object that rings) C E R E __ __ __ __ U M
[part of the brain]

8. (a fixed price) E V A P O __ __ __ __
[change from a liquid to a gas]

9. (cooking vessel) H Y __ __ __ H E S I S
[a careful guess]

10. (edge) E X P E __ __ __ E N T [a scientific test]

11. (play a part) B __ __ __ E R I A [germs]

12. (take the bus)
S O D I U M   C H L O __ __ __ __ [salt]

13. (walking stick) H U R R I __ __ __ __
[a powerful storm]

14. (let fall) H Y __ __ __ __ O N I C S
[the science of farming without soil]

15. (in this place) A T M O S P __ __ __ __
[the air surrounding the Earth]

16. (pocket bread) P R E C I __ __ __ __ T I O N
[rain, snow, sleet, etc.]

17. (burrowing animal) __ __ __ __ C U L E S
[tiny bits of matter]

18. (endure) S A N D B __ __ __ __ I N G
[method of cleaning stone buildings]

19. (shopping area) S __ __ __ __ P O X
[serious contagious disease]

20. (almond or pecan) __ __ __ R I E N T S
[food elements needed for growth]

Answer on page 116.

Scientific Research #2

To find the word that fits each clue, cross off some letters in the scientist's name to the right, and read the remaining letters from left to right.

Example: Goal   <u>AIM</u>   A S̶ I M Q̶ X̶

Clue	Answer	Scientist
1. Smart person	_____	BRATTAIN
2. Secret agent	_____	SPERRY
3. Rabbit	_____	HARVEY
4. Price	_____	COUSTEAU
5. Shade of color	_____	HUBBLE
6. Swimming place	_____	LEAKEY
7. Ache	_____	PAULING
8. Face part	_____	CHAPIN
9. Adult male	_____	MARCONI
10. "Bagged" drink	_____	TESLA
11. Yellow veggie	_____	COPERNICUS
12. Fib	_____	LISTER
13. Squiggly fish	_____	ZEPPELIN
14. Half of twenty	_____	EINSTEIN
15. Grassy area	_____	LAWRENCE
16. Car fuel	_____	GOETHALS

Answer on page 126.

— 2 —

Tricky Cosmic Mysteries

Congratulations! You've successfully made it to the next round of puzzles. Dr. Dunkendorf and I are breathing a little bit easier!

I see it's now time to put your astronomical knowledge of the Earth and sky to the test. In this section, you'll find that Krypton isn't just the name of Superman's planet, and that the universe is full of heavenly bodies. These puzzles may be a bit more difficult, but I'll be right back to help you out. Have a blast!

Our Precious World

Find the word or phrase that completes each sentence below in the same-numbered row in the grid at right. Cross out the answer, letter by letter (all the letters will be next to each other). There will be extra letters on each line. When you are finished, write these leftover letters in the blanks at the bottom of the page. Work from left to right and top to bottom, to find an important message.

1. Disposal areas for garbage are called ___.
2. Animals or plants that no longer exist are ___.
2. Some chemicals are poisonous, or ___.
3. Dense tropical areas are called ___ ___.
4. The part of the atmosphere that blocks out the sun's harmful rays is the ___ ___.
5. Coal and oil formed by the remains of ancient life are called ___ ___.
6. Species that are in peril of dying out completely are ___.
7. A dry area like the Sahara is a ___.
7. The skeletal material that makes up a reef is called ___.
8. The oldest U.S. national park is ___.
9. The gradual increase of the earth's temperature is called global ___.

1	P	R	L	A	N	D	F	I	L	L	S	O	T
2	E	X	T	I	N	C	T	E	T	O	X	I	C
3	R	A	I	N	F	O	R	E	S	T	S	C	T
4	T	H	O	Z	O	N	E	L	A	Y	E	R	E
5	E	F	O	S	S	I	L	F	U	E	L	S	A
6	R	E	N	D	A	N	G	E	R	E	D	T	H
7	S	D	E	S	E	R	T	R	C	O	R	A	L
8	Y	E	L	L	O	W	S	T	O	N	E	E	S
9	W	A	R	M	I	N	G	O	W	A	T	E	R
10	U	U	L	T	R	A	V	I	O	L	E	T	R
11	E	R	O	S	I	O	N	C	S	O	L	A	R
12	E	S	S	O	L	I	D	W	A	S	T	E	S

9. The liquid needed for plant and animal life is ___.

10. The rays of the sun that cannot be seen are ___ rays.

11. The wearing away of soil or rock is called ___.

11. The use of the sun to heat a house is known as ___ energy.

12. Some of the materials in sewers are called ___ ___.

Hidden message ___ ___ ___ ___ ___ ___ ___

___ ___ ___   ___ ___ ___ ___ ___ ' ___

___ ___ ___ ___ ___ ___ ___ ___

Answer on page 117.

Museum Guide

In the write-it-yourself travel guide for an outdoor museum below, some words have blank spaces in them, followed by a number in parentheses ( ). Fill in the blanks by reading the clue on the page at right that matches the number given. Write the answer word in the same-numbered space.

Example: The answer to clue number 1 "Opposite of against" is FOR, so write FOR in the blank spaces for (1) below, to spell CaliFORnia.

In Northern Cali __ __ __ nia (1), a special attraction called Monterey Bay National __ __ rine (2) Sanctuary gets millions of vi __ __ __ ors (3) a year. The tourists watch otters, harbor seals and birds that splash on the b __ __ __ __ es (4). T__ __ __ __ y-six (5) species of aquatic mammals live in the sanctuary, including bottle __ __ __ __ (6) dolphins. There are also many types of inverte __ __ __ __ es (7).

A popular feature is the undersea __ __ __ yon (8). Some things to see are sea otters, who dive under the surface to find creatures like abal __ __ __ (9), and sea ur __ __ __ __ s (10). Otters are closely related to w __ __ __ __ __ __ __ (11). They were al__ __ __ __ (12) wiped out in the early 1900s by fur t __ __ __ pers (13), but they were put on the U.S. En __ __ __ __ __ __ ed (14) Species List and are now making a comeback. You can also watch the seals zip a __ __ __ __ (15) under-water where they s __ __ __ __ (16) up crabs and fast-swimming fish. Another creature to watch, the male cormor__ __ __ (17), dives into the water looking for __ __ __ erials (18) for nest-building.

To catch fresh fish, __ __ __ __ __ ies (19) of herring gulls come to the shoreline. But when they are inland these gulls are s __ __ __ __ ngers (20) and hang out near landf __ __ __ s (21). There are also fish species that feed on __ __ __ __ __ fish (22) and plank __ __ __ (23) at the shoreline.

The Monterey Bay sanctuary is a very valuable center for study and should be pre __ __ __ __ __ d (24) and protected. If you do visit this special museum, you're sure to have a __ __ __ derful (25) time.

Clues

1. Opposite of against
2. Pa's wife
3. Opposite of stand
4. Every
5. Left
6. Organ of smell
7. Pain-in-the-neck kid
8. Soup holder
9. The first number
10. Part of the lower face
11. Artists paint on these
12. Opposite of least
13. Hip-hop music
14. Peril
15. Opposite of short
16. Chicken house
17. Insect
18. Small rug
19. A mark like this :
20. Underground home
21. Sick
22. It goes with peanut butter
23. A heavy weight
24. Start a tennis game
25. Came in first in a race

Answer on page 126.

Criss-Crossing Trees

Place the name of each tree into the one spot where it fits in the grid. Cross off each tree after you position it. One word has been filled in to get you going.

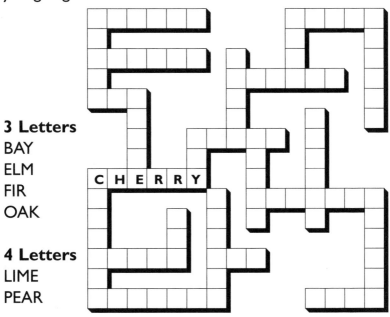

3 Letters
BAY
ELM
FIR
OAK

4 Letters
LIME
PEAR

5 Letters
APPLE
BEECH
CEDAR
ELDER
MAPLE
OLIVE
PECAN

6 Letters
ALMOND
~~CHERRY~~
LAUREL
MIMOSA
NUTMEG
ORANGE
POPLAR
QUINCE

7 Letters
AVOCADO
CYPRESS
SEQUOIA

Answer on page 117.

Uh-Oh!

Write a letter in the blank space on each line to spell something that can cause a lot of sorrow and suffering. Then read down the *starred* column to find out what these events are called.

```
                        *
            TOR ___ A D O
        B L I Z Z ___ R D
    W I N D S ___ O R M
            H ___ R R I C A N E
            E A ___ T H Q U A K E
            G ___ L E
            F ___ O O D

            ___ E L U G E
        W H ___ R L W I N D
        T W I ___ T E R
        S Q U ___ L L
    T E M P E ___ T
            ___ Y P H O O N
    C Y C L O N ___
            ___ I P T I D E
    L A N D ___ L I D E
```

Answer on page 127.

Inside Outer Space

Each sentence below contains a word that is associated with the science of astronomy, but it is hidden. Underline each word when you find it. Ignore the spacing and any punctuation in the sentence.

Example: IS THE BRON<u>COS' MOS</u>COW
TRIP CANCELLED?

1. THERE ARE SEVEN USED CARS IN THE DRIVEWAY.
2. WHO WANTS A TURNOVER FOR DESSERT?
3. DID YOU HEAR THAT JOKE ABOUT THE CIRCUS CLOWN?
4. PLEASE COME TO MY PARTY.
5. WE'LL VISIT THE ALAMO ON FRIDAY.
6. TIME TO WORK ON YOUR GRAMMAR, SON.
7. HE'S AN INEPT, UNEDUCATED RAT!
8. THE STATION IS JUST AROUND THE CORNER.
9. AL PACINO VACATIONED THERE.
10. THIS UNUSUAL PAINTING IS ON SALE.
11. THE PLANE TAXIED DOWN THE RUNWAY.

Answer on page 118.

Spaced Out

What's round and purple and orbits the sun? Find the answer to this riddle by completing the sentences below. Fill in the two missing letters in the words below, then read down the column *two letters at a time*.

1. All space explorations start from ___.
2. The eighth planet from the sun is ___.
3. The water landing of a spacecraft is a ___.
4. The spaceship is driven by a jet ___.
5. Scientists use telescopes at an ___.
6. 10, 9, 8, 7, 6, 5, 4, 3, 2, 1 . . . ___.
7. Rockets go into orbit from a ___.
8. Astronauts measure temperatures in ___.
9. Astronauts ride in the ___.
10. On space trips astronauts do lots of ___.

1. EAR _ _
2. N _ _ TUNE
3. SP _ _ SHDOWN
4. ENGI _ _
5. OBSERVA _ _ RY
6. LI _ _ OFF
7. LAUNC _ _ R
8. DE _ _ EES
9. C _ _ SULE
10. R _ _ EARCH

Answer on page 126.

Astronaut's Hangout

Write a letter in the blank space on each line to complete a word or phrase that is meaningful to an astronaut. Then read down the *starred* column to answer this riddle: What is an astronaut's favorite place on a computer?

```
                    *
            AS ___ EROID
        BLACK ___ OLE
            N ___ BULA
        UNIVER ___ E
              ___ LANET
          GAL ___ XY
              ___ OMET
          MET ___ ORITE

           OR ___ IT
            S ___ TELLITE
            C ___ ATER
```

Answer on page 124.

Seeing Stars

The names of 10 constellations are scattered around this page. Put them into the grid in alphabetical order and then read down the *starred* column. You'll find the type of scientist who studies stars and other heavenly bodies.

Answer on page 123.

Elementary Fun

Atomic elements are the building blocks of nature. Your job is to rebuild the 20 atomic elements below. Take one of the three-letter words from the right-hand column and put it into an empty space in the lefthand column to name all these elements.

1. __ __ __ I U M	POT
2. __ __ __ B O N	TEN
3. __ __ __ A L T	TAN
4. __ __ __ P E R	EON
5. G __ __ __	NIT
6. I O __ __ __ E	TIN
7. K R Y P __ __ __	BAR
8. __ __ __ H I U M	SOD
9. __ __ __ G A N E S E	COP
10. M E R __ __ __ Y	FUR
11. N __ __ __	DIN
12. __ __ __ R O G E N	MAN
13. P L A __ __ __ U M	COB
14. __ __ __ A S S I U M	RAN
15. __ __ __ I U M	OLD
16. S U L __ __ __	LIT
17. T I __ __ __ I U M	CUR
18. T U N G S __ __ __	TON
19. U __ __ __ I U M	CON
20. Z I R __ __ __ I U M	CAR

Answer on page 119.

Material Things

Unscramble each of the numbered words, writing them on the lines provided, then put them into their places on the grid. Read down the *starred* column to see what you should do with this stuff.

1. RISTGN   _____

2. REPPA   _____

3. SLAPCIT   _____

4. TRYTABE   _____

5. NCA   _____

6. LOTBET   _____

7. ZIGEMANA   _____

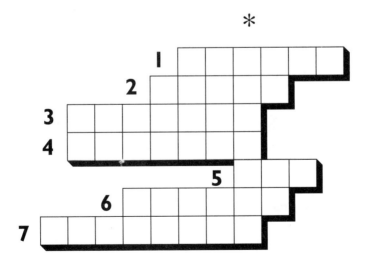

Answer on page 117.

Hot Stuff

Figure out the word that completes each sentence and find it in the same numbered row in the diagram. Cross out the word, letter by letter. All the letters of an answer will always be next to each other, but there will be extra letters on each line. When you are finished, put these leftover letters in the spaces below. Work from left to right and top to bottom, and you'll find the name of a hot place in the United States.

1. You should drink a lot of ___ when you're in hot places.

1. A synonym for dry is ___.

2. A caravan stop in a desert is called an ___.

2. A person who travels from place to place in a desert is a ___.

3. A plant that grows in the desert is a ___ . . .

3. . . . and this plant has a long ___ system.

4. Temperatures in the desert could be very hot, or ___.

5. A ___ , a reptile with scaly skin, is found in warm climates.

1	W	A	T	E	R	D	E	A	R	I	D
2	O	A	S	I	S	A	N	O	M	A	D
3	C	A	C	T	U	S	T	R	O	O	T
4	H	S	C	O	R	C	H	I	N	G	V
5	L	I	Z	A	R	D	A	S	A	N	D
6	L	D	U	N	E	S	M	E	S	A	S
7	F	L	A	S	H	F	L	O	O	D	L
8	W	I	N	D	S	T	O	R	M	S	E
9	C	A	M	E	L	S	Y	G	O	B	I

5. The deserts are filled with ___ ...

6. ... and mounds of this material are called ___.

6. Flat-topped hills in warm places like Arizona are called ___.

7. A short and intense rainfall can lead to a ___ ___.

8. Other dangers in the desert are ___.

9. People travel through the desert on ___.

9. The ___ Desert is in Mongolia and China.

Answer

___ ___ ___ ___ ___

___ ___ ___ ___ ___ ___

Answer on page 120.

Cold Stuff

Figure out the word that completes each sentence and find it in the same numbered row in the diagram. Cross out the word, letter by letter. All the letters of an answer will always be next to each other, but there will be extra letters on each line. When you're finished, put these leftover letters in the spaces below. Work from left to right and top to bottom, and you'll find the name of a very cold place.

1. Water that has been made solid by cold temperatures is called ___ .

1. The ___ is the coldest part of the refrigerator.

2. Black-and-white sea birds that live in cold places are called ___ .

3. A ___ is a huge mass of ice that has formed over many years.

3. ___ is a form of winter precipitation.

4. It can get very cold in the state of ___ .

4. Many people enjoy skiing in the Swiss ___ .

5. ___ have flippers and live in cold ocean waters.

5. Large pieces of floating ice are called ___ .

6. The area at one end of the Earth's axis is the

   ___ ___ .

7. ___ are very large mammals that look like a fish . . .

1	I	C	E	C	F	R	E	E	Z	E	R	O
2	N	P	E	N	G	U	I	N	S	T	I	N
3	G	L	A	C	I	E	R	E	S	N	O	W
4	A	L	A	S	K	A	N	T	A	L	P	S
5	S	E	A	L	S	O	F	L	O	E	S	F
6	S	O	U	T	H	P	O	L	E	A	N	T
7	A	W	H	A	L	E	S	K	R	I	L	L
8	C	R	E	V	A	S	S	E	S	R	C	T
9	I	C	S	A	T	E	L	L	I	T	E	S
10	B	L	U	E	A	B	L	U	B	B	E	R

7. . . . and the main food that they eat is called ___ .

8. Deep cracks in the row 3 items are called ___ .

9. ___ are bodies that circle the earth and give weather information.

10. When you're very cold you might turn ___ .

10. ___ is the fat of row 5 and 7 mammals.

Answer

___ ___ ___ ___ ___ ___ ___ ___ ___

___ ___

___ ___ ___ ___ ___ ___ ___ ___ ___ ___ .

Answer on page 125.

Constellation Find

There are 88 recognized constellations (clusters of stars). To find out the names of some of them, figure out the 3-letter word described by the clue in the parentheses ( ). Write that word in the blank spaces on each line.

1. __ __ __ R O M E D A (also)
2. __ __ __ T E S (scary word said on Halloween)
3. C A M E L O __ __ __ D A L I S (fixed golf score)
4. __ __ __ C E R (metal food container)
5. __ __ __ R I C O R N (hat)
6. __ __ __ I N A (automobile)
7. C __ __ __ A E L E O N (sandwich meat)
8. C __ __ __ E R (large rodent)
9. __ __ __ I N I (valuable stone)
10. __ __ __ S A (male adults)
11. M I C R O S __ __ __ I U M (police officer)
12. O C __ __ __ S (light brown color)
13. P E __ __ __ U S (fuel for automobiles)
14. P __ __ __ N I X (gardener's tool)
15. __ __ __ I T T A R I U S (droop)
16. S E R __ __ __ S (writing tool)

Answer on page 123.

— 3 —

Are You the Codemaster?

XLB HGR YXQB PGL QGLB?

No, it's not a strange foreign language, but a type of puzzle called a cryptogram. In a cryptogram, one letter substitutes for another, so the above question actually says, "Are you game for more?" We hope you are, as time is running out!

See if you can master cryptograms and the other secret code puzzles that are waiting for you in this section of the challenge book. Who knows—you may become so good at them that you can develop your own secret codes to share with your friends. So let's get cracking!

Work Outfits

To find out about some work outfits, change each letter in the codes below to the letter that comes 2 spaces after it in the alphabet. To do this, think of the alphabet as being in a circle and count two letters past the coded letter. For example, Y would be changed to A. This alphabet circle will help you find the right letters. Write the new words on the lines.

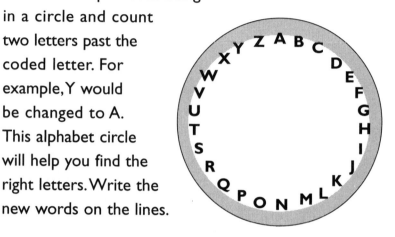

BSPGLE Y QNYAC KGQQGML

_____

YQRPMLYSRQ KYW JCYTC RFC

_____

QNYACQFGN.

_____ .

RFGQ QNYACUYJI GQ

_____

AYJJCB CVRPY TCFGASJYP

_____

YARGTGRW (MP CTY).

_____ .

RFC YQRPMLYSRQ UCYP

_____

QNYAC QSGRQ RFYR AMLRPMJ

_____

RFCGP CLTGPMLKCLR QM

_____

RFCW FYTC YGP RM

_____

ZPCYRFC, RCKNCPYRSPC

_____

AMLRPMJ, YLB

_____

NPCQQSPGXYRGML RM FMJB

_____

RFCGP ZMBGCQ RMECRFCP.

_____ .

Answer on page 117.

Squish Squash

There are two related words on each line. All the letters are in the correct order, but the words are squished together. You have to separate them to find the two terms. There's a clue given with each set of words, for example:

Medical students: I R E N S I D T E R N E N T
= INTERN and RESIDENT

1. Vegetables: L C A E T B B T U A G E C E

= _____

2. Stomach: B A B E L D O L Y M E N

= _____

3. Gases: H E R A L I D U M O N

= _____

4. Endangered species: C O W O N D L O R S V E S

= _____

5. Diseases: M E M U A S L M E S P S

= _____

6. Senses: T A T S O T U E C H

= _____

7. Metals: Z N I C I N K E L C

= _____

8. Cats: S I P A E R M S I A E S E N

= _____

9. Grazing land: M P A S E A D T U O R E W

= _____

10. Apes: G G O I R I B L B L O N A

= _____

11. Planets: M J U E P I R C T U R Y E R

= _____

12. Water parts: H Y O X Y D R G E N O G E N

= _____

13. Oceans: P A I N C I F D I A I C N

= _____

14. Snakes: C O P Y N S T R T H I C T O R O N

= _____

15. Eye parts: L P E U N P S I L

= _____

16. Carbohydrates: S T S U A R C G A R H

= _____

17. Fruits: T A C A N T N G E A L R I O U N E P

E = _____

18. Nuts: P I S F I T A L B C H I O E R T

= _____

Answer on page 120.

Number Switch

Replace each numeral in the coded messages below with the letter it represents (given in the decoder box) and you'll find an interesting fact about one of the elements. Write the decoded words on the lines provided for each message.

A = 1	D = 2	E = 3
F = 4	G = 5	H = 6
I = 7	L = 8	M = 9
N = 10	O = 11	R = 12
S = 13	T = 14	U = 15
	Y = 16	

13 15 8 4 15 12   7 13

_____

4 11 15 10 2   7 10

_____

9 3 1 14,   4 7 13 6,

---

1 10 2   3 5 5 13   1 10 2

---

7 13   10 3 3 2 3 2

---

4 11 12   6 3 1 8 14 6 16

---

6 1 7 12   1 10 2

---

10 1 7 8 13.

Answer on page 123.

Intersecting Symbols

In the strange-looking grid below, some letters of the alphabet meet at the intersection of two symbols, one in the Across row and one in the Down column. (For example: the letter A is found at the intersection of ✳ in the Down column and + in the Across row.) Find each intersection point below and change it to the letter it represents to read a riddle and its answer.

	*	!	@	#	$
+	A	D	E	F	H
/	I	L	N	O	P
=	R	S	T	U	W

Riddle

$= $+   *+   @=   */   !=

_____

@= $+   @+

_____

#+ */ !/ @= $+ */ @+ != @=

$= #/ *= !+   */ @/

@= $+ @+

$= #/ *= !/ !+ ?

Answer

$/ #/ !/ !/ #= @= */ #/ @/

Answer on page 119.

Scrambled Fact

Unscramble each individual word by putting the letters in the right order. Write the new words you make on the lines below and you will learn some interesting information.

DRISB LONY PLEES NI STENS

_____

HEWN HEYT REA VANGHI

_____

SIBBEA. TA THERO MISTE HYTE

_____

SPEEL NAY CELPA. HYET NAC

_____

ZODE NO RETE CHANBERS;

_____

YETH ANC PELSE HELIW

_____

NATGINDS TA HET CHABE RO

_____

HEWN HYET REA GLYNIF. HEYT

_____

REA BLEA OT OD SIHT

_____

CABSUEE NEO LFAH FO HITER

_____

RANIB PESELS NAD HET THROE

_____

LAFH SI AKEWA.

_____ Answer on page 120.

Leather/Middles
Weather Riddles

Change the underlined letter in each word to make a new word. If your words are correct you'll find MIDDLES/RIDDLES and their answers on the topic of LEATHER/WEATHER. Write the new words on the lines provided.

1. WH_I_T _H_ID _S_HE D_A_RT S_O_Y _T_HEN

_____

I_S_ R_U_INED? _O_F TH_U_S _S_EEPS U_S_,

_____

M_E_ _F_AME I_T_ M_A_D.

_____

2. _T_HAT _T_O YO_N_ _C_ELL I_N_ W_R_EN I_F_

_____

_G_AINS _T_HICKENS _E_ND D_O_CKS?

_____

_H_OWL _L_EATHER.

_____

3. CHAT DIM TIE FORTH WAND SAT

_____

DO SHE MOUTH BIND IT TOE SMART

_____

IF SHE PACE? OR SOUR PARK, GEL

_____

SIT, BROW!

_____

4. WHET DIE ORE RAIL CROP DAY DO

_____

THY ETHER GAIN DRIP? BY PROP

_____

AS DIGGER THAT DOUR CLOP.

_____

5. THAT MIND IF STORES GO START

_____

BIDS BIKE? DRAIN STORES.

_____

Answer on page 124.

Job Search

Join two word pieces from the box to make a 6-letter answer to each numbered clue. Write it downward in the grid, and cross off each piece. The starred rows of the completed grid will reveal a scientist's co-worker.

ANS	BAS	CAT	COL	ECT
ING	LIE	MAN	MON	NIP
NTS	OBJ	ORG	PLA	RCH
SET	STA	THS	TRU	TYP

	1	2	3	4	5	6	7	8	9	10
★										
★										

1. Subject of botanists
2. Droopy eared hound
3. A real thing
4. May and June
5. Hearts and livers
6. Treat for a kitten
7. Food substance in potatoes and rice
8. A dog like Lassie
9. President Harry S. ___
10. Using a keyboard

Answer on page 121.

Letter Switch

To find a riddle, change each letter below to the letter that comes one space before it in the alphabet. Write the words on the lines.

X I B U   J T   U I F   C F T U

_____

X B Z   U P   D B U D I   B

_____

T R V J S S F M ?

_____

To find the answer to this riddle, change each letter to the one that comes two spaces before it in the alphabet. Write the words on the lines.

E N K O D   W R   C   V T G G

_____

C P F   C E V   N K M G   C

_____

P W V .

_____

Tip: If you have trouble, the alphabet circle on page 46 may be a help.

Answer on page 117.

Name Dropping

Follow carefully the set of instructions under the grid below to find the first name of a famous scientist.

B	Y	D	M	C	R	Y	C
Z	M	E	E	R	Z	M	F
A	R	D	D	L	D	F	A
E	A	X	C	G	Y	O	Y
R	U	R	D	A	X	R	Z
C	R	M	B	M	B	Z	C
B	R	B	D	I	R	D	Y
R	M	S	G	B	D	X	B

1. Cross off the first seven letters of the alphabet every time you see them.
2. Cross off the last three letters of the alphabet every time you see them.
3. Cross off the 13th letter of the alphabet every time you see it.
4. Cross off the 18th letter of the alphabet every time you see it.
5. Write the unused letters on the blank spaces. Keep the letters in order, from left to right and top to bottom.

___ ___ ___ ___ ___

Now follow the instructions below this grid to find the last name of the scientist.

g	f	f	h	V	K	O	P
Q	A	W	Q	L	i	V	W
K	Q	S	T	K	V	g	b
i	W	L	c	Q	i	J	h
V	E	W	h	Q	x	L	m
Q	K	J	L	W	Q	i	K
h	Q	V	U	L	V	L	W
V	d	J	J	R	W	V	n

1. Cross off the 10th, 11th, and 12th letters of the alphabet every time you see them.
2. Cross off all the lower-case small letters every time you see them.
3. Cross off every **O**.
4. Cross off every **Q**.
5. Cross off the 22nd and 23rd letters every time you see them.
6. Write the unused letters on the blank spaces. Keep the letters in order, from left to right and top to bottom.

—— —— —— —— —— ——

Answer on page 122.

1-2-3

Find a riddle and its answer in 3 easy steps.

1. Solve each math problem.
2. Refer to the code in the box below and replace the numbered answer with the letter it represents.
3. Read each column from top to bottom. We did one to start you off.

A = 4	**H = 12**	**R = 27**
B = 5	**I = 15**	**S = 30**
C = 6	**L = 18**	**T = 35**
D = 8	**M = 20**	**U = 36**
E = 9	**N = 21**	**W = 40**
G = 10	**O = 24**	**Y = 45**

$10 \times 4 =$ __40__ = __W__ $75 - 40 =$ ___ = ___

$6 \times 2 =$ ___ = ___ $4 \times 3 =$ ___ = ___

$9 \times 5 =$ ___ = ___ $3 \times 3 =$ ___ = ___

$9 \times 3 =$ ___ = ___

$25 - 10 =$ ___ = ___ $10 \times 2 =$ ___ = ___

$60 - 30 =$ ___ = ___ $8 \times 3 =$ ___ = ___

$40 \div 2 =$ ___ = ___

$18 - 14 =$ ___ = ___ $18 \div 2 =$ ___ = ___

$70 \div 2 =$ ___ = ___

$8 + 1 =$ ___ = ___

$67 - 40 =$ ___ = ___

95 − 60 = ___ = ___   3 x 5 = ___ = ___
96 − 84 = ___ = ___   37 − 2 = ___ = ___
81 ÷ 9 = ___ = ___

24 ÷ 2 = ___ = ___
4 x 5 = ___ = ___   24 ÷ 6 = ___ = ___
12 x 2 = ___ = ___   60 ÷ 2 = ___ = ___
90 ÷ 3 = ___ = ___
90 − 55 = ___ = ___   10 x 3 = ___ = ___
48 ÷ 2 = ___ = ___

72 − 63 = ___ = ___
4 x 2 = ___ = ___   80 ÷ 4 = ___ = ___
9 x 4 = ___ = ___   40 ÷ 10 = ___ = ___
4 + 2 = ___ = ___   63 ÷ 3 = ___ = ___
16 ÷ 4 = ___ = ___   90 ÷ 2 = ___ = ___
85 − 50 = ___ = ___
45 − 36 = ___ = ___   18 − 10 = ___ = ___
16 − 8 = ___ = ___   90 − 81 = ___ = ___
90 ÷ 9 = ___ = ___
33 + 2 = ___ = ___   54 ÷ 2 = ___ = ___
9 + 3 = ___ = ___   79 − 70 = ___ = ___
30 ÷ 2 = ___ = ___   72 ÷ 8 = ___ = ___
7 x 3 = ___ = ___   15 x 2 = ___ = ___
50 ÷ 5 = ___ = ___

14 + 1 = ___ = ___
30 − 9 = ___ = ___

16 − 12 = ___ = ___

9 x 2 = ___ = ___
24 − 20 = ___ = ___
25 ÷ 5 = ___ = ___   **?**

Answer on page 116.

Circulation Fact

Write the answer to each clue on the numbered spaces. Move the numbered letters to the same-numbered spaces in the answer section to find an important fact about circulation.

Clues

A. Type of school for three-year-olds

$\overline{}\ \overline{}\ \overline{}\ \overline{}\ \overline{}\ \overline{}\ \overline{}$
19 22 7 47 56 61 51

B. Tossed veggie dish __ __ __ __ __
54 44 64 40 20

C. Belonging to me __ __ __ __
57 25 9 16

D. Twelve o'clock __ __ __ __
27 31 4 41

E. Move like a worm __ __ __ __ __ __
52 62 10 15 2 26

F. Chore __ __ __ __
30 63 39 45

G. Cures __ __ __ __ __
33 46 50 37 11

H. Precise __ __ __ __ __
60 13 48 35 28

I. Not tight __ __ __ __ __
38 12 3 65 34

J. Ties up (rhymes with "minds")

$\overline{}\ \overline{}\ \overline{}\ \overline{}\ \overline{}$
1 8 17 42 29

K. Cuckoo (rhymes with "catty")

$\overline{6}$ $\overline{18}$ $\overline{23}$ $\overline{59}$ $\overline{14}$

L. Be present at an event

$\overline{58}$ $\overline{55}$ $\overline{3}$ $\overline{36}$ $\overline{21}$ $\overline{5}$

M. Small lump on the skin

$\overline{49}$ $\overline{53}$ $\overline{24}$ $\overline{32}$

Answer

$\overline{1}$ $\overline{2}$ $\overline{3}$ $\overline{4}$ $\overline{5}$ $\overline{6}$ $\overline{7}$ $\overline{8}$ $\overline{9}$ $\overline{10}$ $\overline{11}$

$\overline{12}$ $\overline{13}$ $\overline{14}$ $\overline{15}$ $\overline{16}$ $\overline{17}$ $\overline{18}$ $\overline{19}$ $\overline{20}$

$\overline{21}$ $\overline{22}$ $\overline{23}$ $\overline{24}$ $\overline{25}$ $\overline{26}$ $\overline{27}$ $\overline{28}$ $\overline{29}$ $\overline{30}$ $\overline{31}$

$\overline{32}$ $\overline{33}$ $\overline{34}$ $\overline{35}$ $\overline{36}$ $\overline{37}$ $\overline{38}$ $\overline{39}$ $\overline{40}$ $\overline{41}$ $\overline{42}$

$\overline{43}$ $\overline{44}$ $\overline{45}$ $\overline{46}$ $\overline{47}$ $\overline{48}$ $\overline{49}$ $\overline{50}$ $\overline{51}$

$\overline{52}$ $\overline{53}$ $\overline{54}$ $\overline{55}$ $\overline{56}$

$\overline{57}$ $\overline{58}$ $\overline{59}$ $\overline{60}$ $\overline{61}$ $\overline{62}$ $\overline{63}$ $\overline{64}$ $\overline{65}$

Answer on page 118.

Filling Station #1

An interesting science fact is hidden here. To find it, figure out the answer to each clue. Then write that word in two places—after the clue and again in the numbered blanks in the page at right, being careful to match-up the numbers. Work back and forth between the clues and the "filling station." One word has been entered for you.

Clues

1, 2, 3, 4 = Vegetable on the cob **CORN**

5, 6, 7, 8 = Fiber used to make rope _____

9, 10, 11, 12 = A fixed price _____

13, 14, 15, 16 = Every _____

17, 18, 19 = A woman who lives in a convent _____

20, 21, 22 = Color of beets _____

23, 24, 25, 26 = Soil _____

27, 28, 29 = Mist _____

30, 31, 32 = Male child _____

33, 34, 35 = Allow _____

36, 37 = Opposite of out _____

38, 39, 40 = Letter after ess _____

41, 42, 43, 44 = End of the arm _____

45, 46, 47 = Definite article _____

Filling Station

IN C̲A L I F O̲ R̲ N̲ IA   T __ __
  1   2 3 4   5 6

T E __ __ E __ __ __ U R __
   7 8   9 10 11   12

R __ __ __ __ E D   O __ E
  13 14 15 16   17

H __ __ D __ __ __   A N __
  18 19 20 21 22   23

T H __ __ __ Y- __ __ U R   D E __ R E E __
   24 25 26 27 28   29   30

__ __ J U __ Y T __ N __ H
31 32   33   34 35

N __ __ E __ __ __ N __ U N D R E D
  36 37 38 39 40   41

__ __ __ __ __ I R T __ E N.
42 43 44 45 46   47

Answer on page 119.

Cute Critter

Change each letter below to the letter that comes immediately before it in the alphabet and you'll find a piece of information about a critter you probably never heard about. Write the new words on the lines.

B X B U F S C F B S J T B

_____

U J O Z D S F B U V S F

_____

O P C J H H F S U I B O

_____

P O F H S B J O P G T B O E .

_____

X I F O J U D B O O P U

_____

G J O E X B U F S J U

_____

T U P Q T F B U J O H ,

_____

N P W J O H , B O E

_____

C S F B U I J O H , B O E

_____

T F F N T U P   C F E F B E .

_____

C V U X I F O T D J F O U J T U T

_____

B E E X B U F S U P J U ,

_____

U I F U J O Z B O J N B M

_____

D P N F T C B D L U P

_____

M J G F .

_____

Answer on page 125.

Intersecting Numbers

In the grid below some letters of the alphabet meet at the intersection of 2 numbers, one in the Across row and one in the Down column. Example: the letter A meets at the intersection of 1 in the Down column and 7 in the Across row. Change each intersection point to the letter it represents to read a riddle and its answer. Write the letters on the lines.

	1	2	3	4	5	6
7	A	C	D	E	F	G
8	H	I	K	N	O	P
9	R	S	T	U	W	Y

Riddle

59 18 17 39   37 58   69 58 49

_____

67 47 39   28 57   69 58 49

_____

27 19 58 29 29   17

_____

38 17 48 67 17 19 58 58

---

17 48 37   17

---

19 17 27 27 58 58 48 ?

Answer

17   57 49 19

---

27 58 17 39   59 28 39 18

---

68 58 27 38 47 39 29 .

Answer on page 116.

Coded Riddle

Use this code to read a riddle and its answer. Write the words on the lines.

A = ■   H = !   M = ✦   R = &
C = @   I = ♣   N = #   S = ✪
D = %   K = ❖   O = ▼   T = ◆
E = ★   L = ✖   P = ✳   V = ●
G = $ W = ✔

✔ ! ★ & ★   % ▼   ✦ ■ & ◆ ♣ ■ # ✪

_____

✖ ★ ■ ● ★   ◆ ! ★ ♣ &

_____

✪ ✳ ■ @   ★ ✪ ! ♣ ✳ ✪ ?

_____

■ ◆   ✳ ■ & ❖ ♣ # $

_____

✦ ★ ◆ ★ ▼ & ✪ .

_____

Answer on page 119.

— 4 —

HOW PUZZLING!

The evil Dr. Frick may not look it, but he's worried. You've done well so far, but he thinks these word puzzles will stop you. Dr. Dunkendorf, on the other hand, is sure you'll make it through this section in no time. See if you can prove him right!

To complete the next group of puzzles, you'll have to figure out how many sides are in a dodecahedron, what part of a chicken nobody wants to eat, and how bears spend their winter vacation. You have to hurry though! So, take a deep breath and turn the page.

Mini Fill-Ins #2

Complete each grid by putting the words into the spaces where they belong.

Fowl

CAPON
CHICKEN
DUCK
HEN
ROOSTER
TURKEY

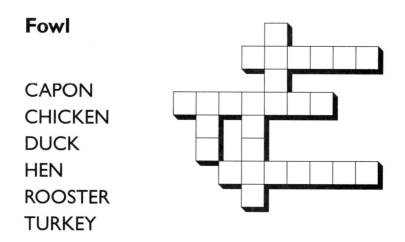

Fungi

MILDEW   MUSHROOM   TRUFFLE
MOLD   TOADSTOOL   YEAST

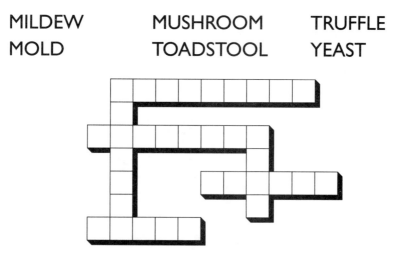

Reptiles

CROCODILE
GECKO
IGUANA
LIZARD
TORTOISE
TURTLE

Cattle

BOVINE   DOGIE
BULL   HEIFER
CALF   STEER
COW

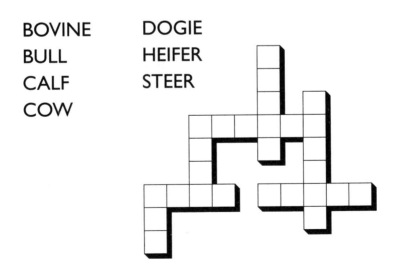

Answer on page 124.

Stormy Scientists

Circle the 18 "angry" words in the grid at right. Look across, up, down, and diagonally, both forward and backward. We've circled **ANGRY** to start you off, and crossed it off the list. When you've circled all the words, put the leftover letters into the blank spaces we've provided. Keep the letters in order (left to right, top to bottom) and you'll answer this riddle: What do astronauts do when they get angry?

Word find

~~ANGRY~~	IRRITATED
BITTER	LIVID
BUGGED	MAD
CROSS	RAGING
DISGUSTED	RILED
FIERCE	SORE
FIERY	TROUBLED
FURIOUS	UPSET
INCENSED	VEXED

```
D R I L E D I V I L
E I D E L B U O R T
S T S G N I G A R F
N B H G F B E Y I I
E I A B U P S E T E
C T N G R S R L A R
N T G S I Y T A T C
I E R S O T O E E E
D R Y F U R M A D F
C R O S S D E X E V
```

Riddle answer

___ ___ ___ ___   ___ ___ ___ ___ ___

___ ___ ___

Answer on page 122.

Scientist's Snack

Write a letter in each blank space to complete the name of some snack foods. Then read downward under the starred column to find the answer to this riddle: What is an atomic scientist's favorite snack?

```
        *
      __ U D G E
  C O O K __ E
      P A __ T R Y
      __ H E R B E T
B R O W N __ E
      P __ P C O R N
  C A __ D Y

      __ A K E
  D O U G __ N U T
      L __ C O R I C E
      __ R E T Z E L
  B I __ C U I T
```

Answer on page 125.

Cross-Offs

Cross off the words described below. Then read the remaining words from *right to left and bottom to top* to find the answer to this riddle: What happens to grapes that are under a lot of stress?

Cross off...

a. 3 rodents

b. 4 words that start with "W" and end with "N"

c. 3 planets

d. 4 meats

e. 2 synonyms for youngsters

f. 4 zoo animals

g. 3 Olympic medals

h. 3 words that contain only the letters A, C, E, and R

i. 3 types of pasta

j. 3 time words

k. 4 bodies of water

TOMORROW RAISINS LIVER WAN

MOLE WOVEN LAGOON YESTERDAY

INTO BABIES URANUS STEAK CARE

PANTHER VEAL TODAY TURN PLUTO

MOUSE TIGER MACARONI ACRE

AND PORK POND WIN RACE ZITI

TODDLERS ZEBRA LION WRINKLED

SILVER WHEN BRONZE RAT GET

SEA GOLD SPAGHETTI THEY

VENUS LAKE

Answer on page 119.

Throw It Out!

Use the grid below and cross out a word or phrase that names a food or part of a food that you would throw out. Example: On the first line you would cross out ORANGE RIND. There will always be some extra letters left on each line after you cross out these words. When you're done, read the letters remaining letters in the grid from left to right and top to bottom. You will discover the first stage of what goes on at a garbage dump.

M	I	O	R	A	N	G	E	R	I	N	D
C	H	I	C	K	E	N	B	O	N	E	C
R	O	B	A	N	A	N	A	P	E	E	L
A	P	P	L	E	C	O	R	E	B	E	S
C	P	E	A	C	H	P	I	T	R	U	M
B	L	S	T	A	L	E	B	R	E	A	D
M	O	L	D	Y	C	H	E	E	S	E	E
F	O	O	E	G	G	S	H	E	L	L	D
F	I	S	H	B	O	N	E	I	N	T	O
P	O	T	A	T	O	S	K	I	N	T	I
N	Y	C	L	A	M	S	H	E	L	L	B
G	R	A	P	E	S	E	E	D	I	T	S

To find out the rest of what happens at the dump, just read the sentence below from left to right. It may look strange, but all the words are actually in the correct order. You just have to figure out the correct spacing of the words in the sentence, that's all!

THE SEBI TSTH ENTUR

NINT OGAS, APR OCES

SCAL LEDD ECO MPO

SITI ON, ORSIM PLYR

OT TING.

Answer on page 121.

Filling Station #2

To find an interesting science fact hidden here, figure out the answer to each clue below. Then write that word in two places—right after the clue and in the "filling station" grid at right, matching up the numbers. One word has been entered for you.

Clues

1, 2, 3, 4, 5 = Make a statement **UTTER**

6, 7, 8, 9 = Fibs _____

10, 11, 12 = Strawberry color_____

13, 14, 15, 16 = Monthly payment to a landlord

_____

17, 18, 19, 20 = Twelve inches _____

21, 22, 23 = Smack _____

24, 25, 26, 27 = Clean _____

28, 29, 30 = Hearing organ _____

31, 32, 33, 34, 35 = Opposite of wrong _____

36, 37, 38, 39 = Center of an apple _____

40, 41, 42 = Mom's husband _____

43, 44, 45 = Drink that comes in a "bag"

_____

46, 47, 48 = Baby bear _____

49, 50, 51 = Used a chair _____

52, 53, 54 = Female chicken _____

55, 56, 57 = Evergreen tree _____

58, 59, 60 = Sides in a dodecahedron _____

Filling Station

B <u>U</u> T T <u>E</u> R F ___ ___ ___   A ___ ___
 1 2 3 4 5   6 7 8 9   10 11

___ I F F E ___ ___ ___ ___   ___ R ___ M
12   13 14 15 16   17   18

M ___ ___ ___ S   ___ N   ___ ___ O
  19 20 21   22   23 24

W ___ Y ___ .   T ___ ___ Y   ___ ___ E
  25   26   27 28   29 30

B ___ ___ ___ ___ ___ L Y
  31 32 33 34 35

___ O L ___ ___ ___ ___   ___ N ___
36   37 38 39 40   41   42

___ H ___ Y   H ___ V E   ___ L ___ ___ ___
43   44   45   46   47 48 49

___ ___   T ___ E   ___ ___ D   O ___
50 51   52   53 54   55

T H E ___ ___   A N ___ ___ ___ N A E .
     56 57   58 59 60

Answer on page 116.

5s, 6s, 7s, 8s

Insert a letter in the blank space on each line to make a common 5-letter word. Then read down the center column to find the name of a science.

```
TO __ AZ
US __ ER
KA __ AK
ON __ ET
SK __ MP
PR __ VE
HE __ LO
CL __ WN
OU __ HT
MA __ BE
```

. . . again, with 6-letter words

```
PLA __ MA
SCR __ LL
CAT __ HY
SQU __ NT
ROB __ TS
VAL __ EY
CHR __ ME
BEG __ AR
CRA __ ON
```

...now, with 7-letter words

EXH __ UST
PAR __ LEY
INS __ EAD
QUA __ TER
CAB __ OSE
RES __ ECT
ARC __ ERY
ACR __ LIC
BLO __ SOM
DEL __ GHT
CRA __ KLE
MES __ AGE

...last, with 8-letter words

ADO __ TION
AQU __ RIUM
WET __ ANDS
SCH __ DULE
PAN __ RAMA
TRA __ SMIT
FAI __ HFUL
PAL __ MINO
DWE __ LING
THE __ RIES
GAR __ OYLE
PLA __ TIME

Answer on page 123.

Lost Letters

One letter was "lost" from each word in the list before it was put in the grid. Example: STABLE is in the list, but the B was lost and STALE was circled in the grid. To find the lost letters and each new word, look across, up, down, forward, backward, and diagonally. Write the lost letter on the line and circle the new word in the grid. (Note: Don't let a few alternate-answer words trip you up. You won't find them in the grid.) When you've found all the words, read the lost letters from **1** to **29** to answer this riddle: Why are bacteria bad at math?

1. STABLE __**B**__

2. BEACON ___

3. FACULTY ___

4. BOARDER ___

5. DURESS ___

6. THIRSTY ___

7. FEATHER ___

8. STURGEON ___

9. PHEASANT ___

10. FEASTS ___

11. TRYOUT ___

12. CLAMPS ___

13. SPOUT ___

14. COMPLETE ___

15. MORTAL ___

16. MAIZE ___

17. INSPECT ___

18. FLIGHT ___

```
S P E A S A N T S T R S T
U R E W O P L C N G C T H
R B R K L D R E S S O S G
G P E B E L S S P H M A I
E N M N Z S E N O H P F F
O G I Q B T Z I T X E A L
N M T R E A D I N G T U I
M A Z E W L C M M H E L N
B R I D E E O O E V Q T G
T H I R T Y P R N T Z Y R
L T U O R T E V C L A P S
N M Y B W X S M O R A L Z
```

19. FLYING ___

20. TIMBER ___

21. READYING ___

22. POWDER ___

23. COPIES ___

24. SOLVE ___

25. WIRING ___

26. MINDED ___

27. PHONIES ___

28. MENTAL ___

29. BRIDGE ___

Answer on page 126.

Location, Location

Find an 8-letter word meaning a plant or animal that lives on a larger plant or animal. You can do this by locating the letters of this word, one by one. Read the clues, which describe exactly where each letter is located in the grid on the page opposite, and place the letters in the spaces below that match the clue numbers.

1. Above "Y" and below "W"

2. Between "N" and "W"

3. To the right of "Z" and below "J"

4. Diagonally between "X" and "M" (look twice!)

5. Between "B" and "L" and above "M"

6. Below "V" and above "U"

7. Diagonally between "W" and "F" and "H" and "M"

8. Between "X" and "U" and next to "V"

Answer

$\overline{}$ $\overline{}$ $\overline{}$ $\overline{}$ $\overline{}$ $\overline{}$ $\overline{}$ $\overline{}$

 1   2   3   4   5   6   7   8

F	Y	Z	B	S	L	B	F
D	X	W	V	M	Q	W	Z
G	J	K	T	V	N	P	Q
Z	R	H	O	F	H	Y	C
V	H	O	X	G	M	B	J
I	E	D	H	A	Z	Q	X
U	B	C	X	Q	M	V	E
B	N	A	W	K	D	M	U

Answer on page 116.

Going Batty

There's a BAT on each line below and it's part of a longer word. Just fill in the blanks with letters to form words that answer the clues in the parentheses ( ) and you'll be completely BATty!

1. __ __ __ __ B A T (a person good at physical stunts)
2. B A T __ __ __ __ (groups of cookies)
3. B A T __ __ __ __ __ (after-shower wear)
4. B A T __ __ __ (Robin's friend who wears a cape)
5. B A T __ __ (what a twirler twirls)
6. B A T __ __ __ (a cake before it's baked)
7. B A T __ __ __ __ (Walkman energy source)
8. B A T __ __ __ (a fight)
9. B A T __ __ __ __ __ __ __ (a war boat)
10. __ __ B A T __ (verbal contest or discussion)
11. __ __ __ __ B A T __ __ (where a baby chick is hatched)
12. __ __ __ B A T __ __ __ __ (people who tan themselves at the beach)
13. __ __ B A T __ (a refund)
14. __ __ __ B A T __ (a day set aside for worship)

Answer on page 117.

— 5 —

Our Weird, Wonderful World

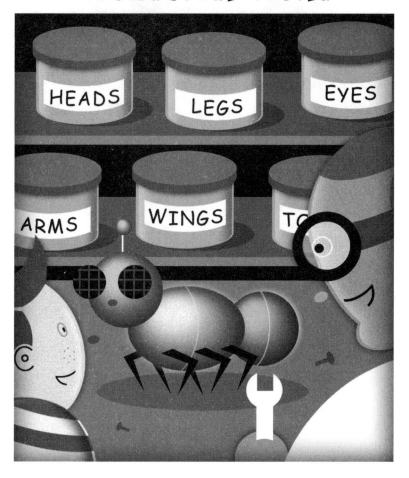

This is it—we're getting close now. By creating creepy creatures, tracking down icky bugs, and smelling a few flowers, saving the world will be a breeze!

Create-a-Creature

Like a really mad scientist, you can create a creature.
Here's the formula: On each line, use the word and
the letter given and scramble all the letters to make
the creature described. Write the creature's name in
the blank spaces. Example: TAG + O = Farm animal
with short horns = GOAT

1. STREAM + H = Small, furry rodent

= _____

2. ORDEAL + P = Wild animal with spots

= _____

3. KIN + M = Animal valued for its fur

=_____

4. RIPE + V = Poisonous snake = _____

5. BRAVE + E = Animal that builds dams

= _____

6. MINER + E = Animal valued for its fur

= _____

7. HERS + W = Very small mouselike animal

= _____

8. UTTER + L = Reptile that travels with its

own house = _____

9. LAME + C = Desert animal with a hump

= _____

10. WINS + E = Pigs or hogs = _____

11. RASH + K = Saltwater fish that's dangerous

to humans = _____

12. LEASE + W = Small animal with thick fur

= _____

13. ROB + A = Wild hog = _____

14. TIRE + G = Striped wild animal _____

15. DOT + A = Animal related to the frog

= _____

16. OPPOSER + I = Sea animal that looks like

a small whale = _____

17. GLEE + A = Bird of prey = _____

18. PENCIL + A = Large bird with a long bill

= _____

19. NEAR + V = Large black bird = _____

20. ROBE + X = Type of dog = _____

21. PLANES + I = Type of dog = _____

22. TICKER + C = Insect with long legs

= _____

23. HOT + M = Insect similar to a butterfly

= _____

24. RAZE + B = Black-and-white-striped animal

= _____

Answer on page 121.

Bug Off!

In the grid on the right, find and circle the names of 17 different insects. Look across, up, down, and diagonally, both forward and backward to find the bugs listed below. APHID has been circled in the grid to start you off.

After you've found and circled all the words, put the leftover letters into the blank spaces we've provided. Keep the letters in order, from left to right and top to bottom, and you'll answer this riddle: What did the proud mother lightning bug say about her son?

Word find

ANT	KATYDID
~~APHID~~	LADYBUG
BEETLE	LOCUST
CICADA	MIDGE
CRICKET	TERMITE
EARWIG	TICK
FRUITFLY	WASP
GNAT	WEEVIL
HORNET	

```
C  H  E  G  U  B  Y  D  A  L
R  I  E  G  I  S  B  P  F  R
I  H  C  T  D  G  H  I  R  E
C  O  G  A  S  I  N  G  U  L
K  R  I  N  D  U  M  A  I  T
E  N  W  T  H  A  C  V  T  E
T  E  R  M  I  T  E  O  F  E
T  T  A  F  I  E  O  R  L  B
H  I  E  C  W  A  S  P  Y  S
A  G  K  A  T  Y  D  I  D  E
```

Riddle answer

__ __ __ __ __ __ __ __

__ __ __ __ __ __ __ __

__ __ __

Answer on page 125.

Ear-ing Aid

Both humans and animals use their ears for hearing. There's an EAR on each line below—part of a longer word. Fill in the blanks with letters to answer the clues—and you'll be able to EAR perfectly!

1. __ __ __ E A R __ __ __ __ = the way a person or thing looks
2. __ E A R __ = hair growth on a man's face
3. __ __ E A R __ __ __ = space in a forest without any trees or bushes
4. E A R __ __ = opposite of late
5. E A R __ __ __ __ = serious and sincere
6. E A R __ __ __ __ __ = jewelry worn on the lobes
7. E A R __ __ __ __ __ __ __ = strong shaking of the ground
8. E A R __ __ __ __ __ __ = small, wriggly creature that lives in the soil
9. __ E A R __ __ __ = closest
10. __ E A R __ __ = round gems found in oysters
11. __ __ __ E A R __ __ __ = practice performance of a play
12. __ __ __ E A R __ __ __ __ = person who studies or tests things
13. __ __ E A R = remove wool from a sheep
14. __ __ E A R = weapon used to catch fish
15. __ __ E A R = make a serious promise
16. __ E A R __ __ __ = ripping

Answer on page 117.

Problem Solving

In the blanks provided, follow the directions on each line very carefully and you'll change a problem for some animals (like bears) into a solution.

1. Write LACK OF FOOD without word spacing

_____

2. Change "A" to the letter after it in the alphabet

_____

3. Change "OFF" to "AT"

_____

4. Change the second vowel to "I"

_____

5. Change the third consonant to "R"

_____

6. Change the fourth consonant to "N"

_____

7. Get rid of the first letter

_____

8. Change the last letter to "N"

_____

9. Place an "E" between the first two consonants

_____

10. Place "HI" before the first letter

_____

Answer on page 120.

Opposite Distraction

Fill in the blank spaces with a word that means the *opposite* of the word inside the brackets [ ] at the left. The new word will name the scientist who did what is described in the parentheses ( ) below.

1. [weak]   A R M __ __ __ __ __ __
   (first person to walk on the moon)
2. [lose]   D A R __ __ __
   (developed theory of evolution)
3. [near]   __ __ __ A D A Y
   (made the first generator)
4. [none]   H __ __ __ E Y
   (discovered comet named after him)
5. [his]   __ __ __ __ C H E L
   (discovered the planet Uranus)
6. [high]   __ __ __ E L L
   (predicted the position of planet Pluto)
7. [sick]   M A X __ __ __ __
   (worked on magnetism)
8. [begin]   M __ __ __ E L
   (did experiments on heredity)
9. [old]   __ __ __ T O N
   (discovered laws of gravity)
10. [future]   __ __ __ __ E U R
    (developed milk sterilization process)
11. [peace]   D E __ __ __
    (first to liquify hydrogen)
12. [left]   W __ __ __ __ __ BROTHERS
    (flew the first airplane)

Answer on page 124.

Creature Body Parts

Here's an amazing scientific discovery. You can add the same two letters to partial words to create a creature and a body part. Just take a two-letter piece from the box below and place it in the blank spaces on each line to make the ending of a creature's name and the beginning of a body part. We did one for you. Cross off each 2-letter piece as you use it.

AB	AD	AN	AR	CH
EY	FE	LE	NA	NE
SP	~~ST~~	TE	TH	TO

1. L O C U / **S T** / O M A C H
2. J A G U / __ __ / M S
3. G I R A F / __ __ / E T
4. C R / __ __ / D O M E N
5. T U R K / __ __ / E B R O W
6. W H A / __ __ / G S
7. S W / __ __ / K L E
8. S A R D I / __ __ / C K
9. F I N / __ __ / I N
10. W A / __ __ / I N E
11. I G U A / __ __ / V E L
12. M O / __ __ / I G H
13. M O S Q U I / __ __ / E S
14. T E R M I / __ __ / E T H
15. T O / __ __ / E N O I D S

Answer on page 125.

Simile Scramble

A simile is a phrase that compares one thing to another using the words "like" or "as." The simile "strong as an ox" suggests that someone has the strength of an ox. Each simile here contains the name of a creature. Unscramble the two capitalized words in each line below to form a common simile. Write the unscrambled words on the lines.

1. PHYAP as a RALK

_____

2. DMA as a HETRON

_____

3. LIBDN as a TAB

_____

4. UGHRYN as a ABRE

_____

5. LYS as a OFX

_____

6. ERD as a BOLREST

_____

7. SOLEO as a SOGOE

_____

8. GRAEE as a REVABE

_____

9. LOWS as a LISAN

_____

10. LEGNET as a MALB

_____

11. LOBD as a NOLI

_____

12. ZARCY as a ONOL

_____

13. ISEW as an OLW

_____

14. UPROD as a COPEKAC

_____

15. ETIQU as a SUMOE

_____

16. TAF as a GPI

_____

17. ABDL as an ALEEG

_____

18. BUNTROBS as a LUME

_____

19. AWKE as a TINKET

_____

20. SYBU as a EEB

_____

Answer on page 124.

Criss-Crossing Fish

Place the name of each fish into the one spot where it will fit in the grid. Cross off each fish after you position it. One word has been filled in to get you going.

3 Letters

COD
EEL
RAY

4 Letters

HAKE
LING
SOLE
TUNA

5 Letters

GUPPY
LOACH
SHARK
SKATE
SPRAT
WAHOO

6 Letters

MARLIN
MINNOW
REDFIN

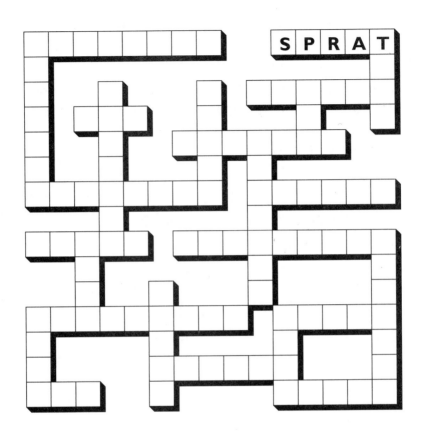

S P R A T

7 Letters

ANCHOVY
LAMPREY
PIRANHA
POMPANO
WALLEYE

8 Letters

ALBACORE
PICKEREL

9 Letters

BARRACUDA
STEELHEAD

Answer on page 120.

Criss-Crossing Body Parts

Place each body part into the diagram in the one spot where it belongs. Cross off each word after you place it, because it will only be used once. We put in a few letters to get you going. Watch out! There are some tricky spots!

3 Letters
ARM
EAR
EYE
LEG
LIP

4 Letters
BONE
HAND
HEAD
KNEE
NAIL
NOSE

5 Letters
AORTA
BRAIN
ELBOW
HEART
LIVER
SPINE
WAIST

6 Letters
FINGER
SPLEEN
THORAX
TONGUE

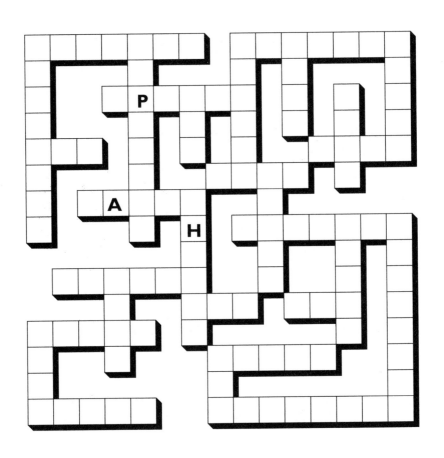

7 Letters

STOMACH

TONSILS

TRACHEA

8 Letters

ADENOIDS

APPENDIX

PANCREAS

SHOULDER

Answer on page 119.

Backing In

Figure out the words that answer the clues given in the parentheses ( ). Write those words in the blank spaces, but write them in *backwards*, to form the name of a flower on each line.

Example: __ __ __ S Y (short sleep)

= P A N S Y (the word NAP, backwards)

1. A M A R Y __ __ __ __ S (sick)

2. A __ __ __ __ O N E (grown-up males)

3. __ __ __ __ E R C U P (bathing place)

4. C A R __ __ __ __ I O N (make animal skins into leather)

5. C L E M A __ __ __ __ (use a chair)

6. D A F F O __ __ __ __ (jar top)

7. __ __ __ __ D E N I A (cleaning cloth)

8. I M __ __ __ __ I E N C E (type of dance)

9. I __ __ __ (title for a man)

10. L A V E N __ __ __ (color of tomatoes)

11. __ __ __ I G O L D (male sheep)

12. __ __ __ F L O W E R (sweet potato)

13. __ __ __ C I S S U S (took part in a race)

14. P E R I W I N __ __ __ (big moose)

15. P E __ __ __ I A (cashew, for example)

16. __ __ __ P Y (another name for Dad)

17. S __ __ __ D R A G O N (cooking utensil)

18. S __ __ __ B A L L (came in first in an election)

19. S W __ __ __ W I L L I A M (with "off," a golfing term)

20. W I S T E __ __ __ (what we breathe)

Answer on page 119.

Transplanted Body Parts

We've taken all the letters of some body-part references and transplanted them into nonsense phrases. Each body part in the left column has a transplanted phrase in the right column. Can you match up all of them like we did for STOMACH and HAM COTS? Note: All the letters in the body part will be used in the transplant.

1. STOMACH __C__
2. BLOODSTREAM ___
3. RIB CAGE ___
4. TRACHEA ___
5. DIAPHRAGM ___
6. ESOPHAGUS ___
7. SKELETON ___
8. LIGAMENTS ___
9. SPINAL CORD ___
10. CRANIUM ___
11. CEREBELLUM ___
12. VENTRICLE ___
13. ALVEOLI ___

A. CLEVER TIN
B. VEAL OIL
C. HAM COTS
D. ME CURE BELL
E. LEOTARD MOBS
F. CARE HAT
G. BIG RACE
H. MAC RUIN
I. GRAPH MAID
J. STING MEAL
K. EEL KNOTS
L. COLD SPRAIN
M. HUGE SOAPS

Answer on page 121.

Creature Words

The name of each creature in the righthand column contains a word that fits the clue in the lefthand column. To find this word, cross off some letters in the creature's name and read the remaining letters from left to right. Write the new words on the blank spaces. We did one for you.

Clue	Answer	Creature
1. Bottom opposite	**TOP**	ANTELOPE
2. Sack		BADGER
3. Ship		BOBCAT
4. Folding bed		COYOTE
5. Tilt		ELEPHANT
6. Material in pencils		LEOPARD
7. Despise		HAMSTER
8. Glass container		JAGUAR
9. Morning riser		SKUNK
10. Man's neckwear		TIGER
11. A direction		WILDEBEEST
12. Labyrinth		CHIMPANZEE
13. Use a barbecue		GORILLA
14. Male child		BISON
15. Sock contents		FERRET
16. Baby's bed		CARIBOU
17. Bus passenger		REINDEER
18. Opposite of light		AARDVARK

Answer on page 125.

Eye Cue

Add one letter to each line to make two new words. The added letter should end the word on the left and begin the word on the right. Example: Put an O on the first line to make CELL**O** and **O**PEN, as we did below. When you're done, read *down* the column to find someone who is an eye specialist. Make sure the letters you add work for both words!

CELL **O** PEN

TRAM __ RICE

PLUS __ AIR

CHAR __ RAIL

FORT __ ILL

SAG __ WAKE

EASE __ ADDER

SPAS __ OTHER

RODE __ WING

GAVE __ EVER

PINT __ PAL

THIN __ HOST

SWAM __ CON

DISCUS __ PRINT

FINES __ RAVEL

Answer on page 122.

— THE PASSWORD! —

This is really it! If you have worked all the puzzles in the book, you now have the key to finding the password we need to save the world from an onslaught of rampaging, out-of-control robots. Just turn the page and complete one final puzzle to learn the secret password that Dr. Dunkendorf forgot. Then we can reset the Zagbar-5000 computer to send a signal to foil Dr. Frick's dastardly plot!

But please hurry! Time is short, and you are our only hope!

Countdown!

To discover the Professor's password, so we can switch the settings on the robots from "Destroy" to "Dance," work out the three-word phrase on the opposite page. Take the indicated letters from all the puzzles you have done and place them in the numbered spaces, counting down to the password—and that's it! Good luck!

On space #14, write the 3rd letter on line 20 from Simile Scramble

On space #13, write lost letter 10 from Lost Letters

On space #12, write the letter in space #56 from Filling Station #2

On space #11, write the last letter on the 2nd line of Material Things

On space #10, write the 3rd letter of the first word in riddle answer from Stormy Scientists

On space #9, write the first letter of the next-to-the last word from Cute Critter

On space #8, write the first letter of answer F from Circulation Fact

On space #7, write the 5th letter of answer 9 from Job Search

On space #6, write the first letter of the first answer word from Scrambled Fact

On space #5, write the first letter of the 7th answer word from Work Outfits

On space #4, write the 4th letter of the second word in Seeing Stars

On space #3, write the 4th letter of the first word in Uh-Oh

On space #2, write the middle letter of answer 2 in the left column of Center Line

On space #1, write the 5th letter of answer 13 in Science Study

The Password

$$\overline{} \quad \overline{} \quad \overline{} \quad \overline{} \qquad \overline{}$$
1   2   3   4   5

$$\overline{} \quad \overline{} \quad \overline{} \quad \overline{} \quad \overline{} \quad \overline{} \quad \overline{} \quad \overline{} \quad \overline{}$$
6   7   8   9   10   11   12   13   14

You've done it! You've saved us all! Now see if you can anagram the letters in the password above into the name of a famous scientist. (But don't miss the celebration on the next page!)

Clue: His full name appears somewhere in this book.

— — — — — —

— — — — — — — —

Answers

A to Z

Examine	**A**sk
Query	O**b**serve
Demand	Scrutinize
Disco**v**er	Explain
Investigate	**I**nquire
Searc**h**	Determine
See**k**	Probe
Quiz	**J**udge
Inspect	**F**igure out
Try	Prove
Sample	Verify
Recognize	Unearth
Study	Revie**w**

Location, Location

P A R A S I T E
1 2 3 4 5 6 7 8

Answer: Pparasite

Stormy Scientists

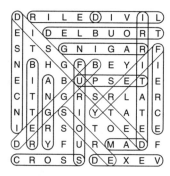

1-2-3

Why is a thermometer the most educated thing in a lab? It has so many degrees.

Intersecting Numbers

What do you get if you cross a kangaroo and a raccoon? A fur coat with pockets.

Filling Station #2

1, 2, 3, 4, 5 = Utter
6, 7, 8, 9 = Lies
10, 11, 12 = Red
13, 14, 15, 16 = Rent
17, 18, 19, 20 = Foot
21, 22, 23 = Hit
24, 25, 26, 27 = Wash
28, 29, 30 = Ear
31, 32, 33, 34, 35 = Right
36, 37, 38, 39 = Core
40, 41, 42 = Dad
43, 44, 45 = Tea
46, 47, 48 = Cub
49, 50, 51 = Sat
52, 53, 54 = Hen
55, 56, 57 = Fir
58, 59, 60 = Ten

Butterflies are different from moths in two ways. They are brightly colored and they have clubs at the end of their antennae.

General Science

1. Inse**ctici**de
2. **Torn**ado
3. Decom**pose**
4. **Shiver**ing
5. Mic**robes**
6. Micro**scope**
7. Cere**bellum**
8. Evapo**rate**
9. Hypo**thesis**
10. Experi**ment**
11. **Bact**eria
12. Sodium chlo**ride**
13. Hurri**cane**
14. **Hydro**ponics
15. Atmos**phere**
16. Preci**pita**tion
17. **Mole**cules
18. Sand**blasting**
19. **Small**pox
20. **Nut**rients

116

Material Things

Answer: Recycle

Work Outfits

During a space mission astronauts may leave the spaceship. This space-walk is called Extra Vehicular Activity (or EVA). The astronauts wear space suits that control their environment so they have air to breathe, temperature control, and pressurization to hold their bodies together.

Our Precious World

1. Landfills	7. Coral
2. Extinct	8. Yellowstone
2. Toxic	9. Warming
3. Rain forests	9. Water
4. Ozone layer	10. Ultraviolet
5. Fossil fuels	11. Erosion
6. Endangered	11. Solar
7. Desert	12. Solid wastes

Answer: Protect the earth's resources

Ear-ing Aid

1. Appearance	9. Nearest
2. Beard	10. Pearls
3. Clearing	11. Rehearsal
4. Early	12. Researcher
5. Earnest	13. Shear
6. Earrings	14. Spear
7. Earthquake	15. Swear
8. Earthworm	16. Tearing

Letter Switch

Riddle: What is the best way to catch a squirrel?

Answer: Climb up a tree and act like a nut.

Criss-Crossing Trees

The Machine Age

Jackhamm **e** r
Ha **r** vester
G enerator
Bulld **o** zer
Turbi **n** e
C **o** pier
Compressor
Typewr **i** ter
C omputer
Fac **s** imile

Answer: Ergonomics

Going Batty

1. Acrobat	8. Battle
2. Batches	9. Battleship
3. Bathrobe	10. Debate
4. Batman	11. Incubator
5. Baton	12. Sunbathers
6. Batter	13. Rebate
7. Battery	14. Sabbath

Inside Outer Space

1. THERE ARE SE<u>VEN US</u>ED CARS IN THE DRIVEWAY.
2. WHO WANTS <u>A TURN</u>OVER FOR DESSERT?
3. DID YOU H<u>EAR THAT</u> JOKE ABOUT THE CIRCUS CLOWN?
4. PLEASE <u>COME T</u>O MY PARTY.
5. WE'LL VISIT THE ALA<u>MO ON</u> FRIDAY.
6. TIME TO WORK ON YOUR GRAM<u>MAR, SON</u>.
7. HE'S AN I<u>NEPT, UN</u>EDUCATED RAT!
8. THE STATION IS J<u>UST AROUND</u> THE CORNER.
9. AL PAC<u>INO VAC</u>ATIONED THERE.
10. THI<u>S UNUS</u>UAL PAINTING IS ON SALE.
11. THE <u>PLANE T</u>AXIED DOWN THE RUNWAY.

Same Starts

1. Venom
   Venus
   Venison
2. Potassium
   Potato
   Potent
3. Metabolism
   Metric
   Method
4. Cancer
   Cannibal
   Canyon
5. Gall bladder
   Gallon
   Galapagos
6. Calcium
   Calories
   Callus
7. Heron
   Herring
   Heredity
8. Everest
   Everglades
   Evergreen
9. Petrified
   Petroleum
   Petri dish
10. Cobalt
    Cobweb
    Cobra
11. Chimpanzee
    Chipmunk
    Chicken pox
12. Starfish
    Starch
    Stamina

Four Close Relatives

1. **Face Parts**
   Jaw
   Mouth
   Cheek
   Lips

2. **Flowers**
   Daisy
   Rose
   Sweet pea
   Lily of the valley

3. **Trees**
   Weeping willow
   Date palm
   Cherry
   Pine

4. **Fruits**
   Grape
   Plum
   Peach
   Apple

5. **Leg Parts**
   Ankle
   Knee
   Foot
   Shin

6. **Arm Parts**
   Wrist
   Hand
   Finger
   Funny Bone

7. **Meats**
   Pork
   Steak
   Veal
   Lamb

8. **Vegetables**
   Peas
   Lima beans
   String beans
   Squash

9. **Body Organs**
   Liver
   Lungs
   Heart
   Brain

Circulation Fact

A. Nursery
B. Salad
C. Mine
D. Noon
E. Wiggle
F. Task
G. Heals
H. Exact
I. Loose
J. Binds
K. Batty
L. Attend
M. Wart

Answer: Blood brings oxygen and nutrients to the cells and takes away waste materials.

Cross-Offs

a. mole, mouse, rat
b. wan, woven, win, when
c. Uranus, Pluto, Venus
d. liver, steak, veal, pork
e. babies, toddlers
f. panther, tiger, zebra, lion
g. silver, bronze, gold
h. care, acre, race
i. macaroni, ziti, spaghetti
j. tomorrow, yesterday, today
k. lagoon, pond, sea, lake

Answer: They get wrinkled and turn into raisins.

Elementary Fun

1. **Bar**ium	11. **Ne**on
2. **Car**bon	12. **Nit**rogen
3. **Cob**alt	13. Plati**num**
4. **Cop**per	14. **Pot**assium
5. **Gold**	15. **Sod**ium
6. **Iod**ine	16. Sul**fur**
7. **Krypton**	17. **Titan**ium
8. **Li**thium	18. Tungs**ten**
9. **Man**ganese	19. U**ran**ium
10. Mer**cury**	20. Zir**con**ium

Criss-Crossing Body Parts

Coded Riddle

Where do Martians leave their spaceships? At parking meteors.

Backing In

1. Amary**llis**	11. **Mar**igold
2. Ane**mone**	12. **May**flower
3. **But**tercup	13. **Nar**cissus
4. Car**nation**	14. Periwin**kle**
5. Clema**tis**	15. Pe**tun**ia
6. Daff**odil**	16. **Poppy**
7. **Gar**denia	17. Snap**dragon**
8. Im**patience**	18. **Snow**ball
9. **Iris**	19. **Sweet** William
10. Laven**der**	20. Wiste**ria**

Filling Station #1

1, 2, 3, 4 = Corn
5, 6, 7, 8 = Hemp
9, 10, 11, 12 = Rate
13, 14, 15, 16 = Each
17, 18, 19 = Nun
20, 21, 22 = Red
23, 24, 25, 26 = Dirt
27, 28, 29 = Fog
30, 31, 32 = Son
33, 34, 35 = Let
36, 37 = In
38, 39, 40 = Tee
41, 42, 43, 44 = Hand
45, 46, 47 = The

In California the temperature reached one hundred and thirty-four degrees on July tenth nineteen hundred and thirteen.

Intersecting Symbols

What is the filthiest word in the world? Pollution

Criss-Crossing Fish

Squish Squash

1. Lettuce/cabbage
2. Belly/abdomen
3. Helium/radon
4. Condors/wolves
5. Measles/mumps
6. Taste/touch
7. Zinc/nickel
8. Siamese/Persian
9. Meadow/pasture
10. Gorilla/gibbon
11. Mercury/Jupiter
12. Hydrogen/oxygen
13. Pacific/Indian
14. Constrictor/python
15. Lens/pupil
16. Starch/sugar
17. Tangerine/cantaloupe
18. Pistachio/filbert

Hot Stuff

1. Water
1. Arid
2. Oasis
2. Nomad
3. Cactus
3. Root
4. Scorching
5. Lizard

5. Sand
6. Dunes
6. Mesas
7. Flash flood
8. Windstorms
9. Camels
9. Gobi

Answer: Death Valley (California)

Science Study

1. **Bio**logy
2. Electromag**net**ism
3. **Cry**ogenics
4. **Dend**rology
5. **Clim**atology
6. **Tax**idermy
7. **Met**allurgy
8. **Arch**aeology
9. **Robo**tics
10. **Astro**nomy
11. Herp**et**ology
12. Ana**tomy**
13. **Bota**ny
14. **Met**eorology
15. **Zoo**logy

Scrambled Fact

Birds only sleep in nests when they
are having babies. At other times
they sleep any place. They can doze
on tree branches; they can sleep
while standing at the beach or when
they are flying. They are able to do
this because one half of their brain
sleeps and the other half is awake.

Problem Solving

1. L A C K O F F O O D
2. L B C K O F F O O D
3. L B C K A T O O D
4. L B C K A T I O D
5. L B R K A T I O D
6. L B R N A T I O D
7. B R N A T I O D
8. B R N A T I O N
9. B E R N A T I O N
10. H I B E R N A T I ON

Some animals (like bears) can't get
enough food in the winter so they
hibernate.

Throw It Out!

The following are crossed out (in order):

Orange rind	Moldy cheese
Chicken bone	Eggshell
Banana peel	Fish bone
Apple core	Potato skin
Peach pit	Clamshell
Stale bread	Grape seed

Grid answer: Microbes crumble food into tiny bits. (Under grid: These bits then turn into gas, a process called decomposition, or simply rotting.)

Center Line

Ans**w** ers	Eme **r** ald
Shr **i** vel	Dep **o** sit
Bli **s** ter	Wel **c** ome
Pal **e** tte	Boo **k** let
Knu **c** kle	
Imp **r** ove	Hat **c** het
Fan **a** tic	Adv **a** nce
Tea **c** her	Gra **n** ite
Man **k** ind	San **d** bar
Pea **s** ant	Cop **y** cat

Answer:
Wisecracks

Answer:
Rock candy

Create-a-Creature

1. Hamster	13. Boar
2. Leopard	14. Tiger
3. Mink	15. Toad
4. Viper	16. Porpoise
5. Beaver	17. Eagle
6. Ermine	18. Pelican
7. Shrew	19. Raven
8. Turtle	20. Boxer
9. Camel	21. Spaniel
10. Swine	22. Cricket
11. Shark	23. Moth
12. Weasel	24. Zebra

Job Search

P	B	O	M	O	C	S	C	T	T
* L	A	B	O	R	A	T	O	R	Y
A	S	J	N	G	T	A	L	U	P
N	S	E	T	A	N	R	L	M	I
* T	E	C	H	N	I	C	I	A	N
S	T	T	S	S	P	H	E	N	G

Answer: Laboratory technician

A Doctor in the House?

1. Pedia**t**rician	9. Surge**on**
2. Or**t**hopedist	10. Chiro**p**odist
3. Derma**t**ologist	11. Dentist
4. Psychiatrist	12. Ortho**d**ontist
5. Obstetrician	13. **R**adiologist
6. Neurolog**i**st	14. **T**oxicologist
7. Parame**d**ic	15. Therapist
8. Nutri**t**ionist	

Transplanted Body Parts

1. C	8. J
2. E	9. L
3. G	10. H
4. F	11. D
5. I	12. A
6. M	13. B
7. K	

Habitats for Scientists

Answer: Rachel Carson (author of "The Sea Around Us" and "Silent Spring")

Stormy Scientists

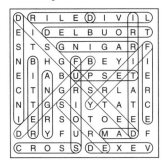

Riddle Answer: They blast off.

Eye Cue

CELL	O	PEN
TRAM	P	RICE
PLUS	H	AIR
CHAR	T	RAIL
FORT	H	ILL
SAG	A	WAKE
EASE	L	ADDER
SPAS	M	OTHER
RODE	O	WING
GAVE	L	EVER
PINT	O	PAL
THIN	G	HOST
SWAM	I	CON
DISCUS	S	PRINT
FINES	T	RAVEL

Answer: Ophthalmologist

Three Close Relatives

1. Dogs
Fox terrier
Great Dane
French poodle

2. Insects
Yellow jacket
Roach
Water bug

3. Fish
Brook trout
Sting ray
Black sea bass

4. Amphibians
Frog
Toad
Newt

5. Mammals
Wild goat
Polar bear
Blue fox

6. Forest Workers
Park ranger
Logger
Wood chopper

7. Plant Parts
Stem
Leaf
Root

8. Birds
Dove
Hawk
Parrot

9. Precipitation
Sleet
Snow
Hail *

10. Metals
Gold
Silver
Copper

11. Snakes
Adder
Viper
Rattler

Name Dropping

Famous scientist: Louis Pasteur

Number Switch

Sulfur is found in meat, fish, and eggs and is needed for healthy hair and nails.

5s, 6s, 7s, 8s

TO P AZ
US H ER
KA Y AK
ON S ET
SK I MP
PR O VE
HEL L O
CL O WN
OU G HT
MA Y BE

Science: Physiology— the study of the functions and activities of living organisms

PLA S MA
SCR O LL
CAT C HY
SQU I NT
ROBO T S
VAL L EY
CHR O ME
BEG G AR
CRA Y ON

Science: Sociology— the study of society and social groups

EXH A UST
PAR S LEY
INS T EAD
QUA R TER
CAB O OSE
RES P ECT
ARC H ERY
ACR Y LIC
BLO S SOM
DEL I GHT
CRA C KLE
MES S AGE

Science: Astrophysics— the study of celestial objects and phenomena

ADO P TION
AQU A RIUM
WET L ANDS
SCH E DULE
PAN O RAMA
TRA N SMIT
FAI T HFUL
PAL O MINO
DWEL L ING
THE O RIES
GAR G OYLE
PLA Y TIME

Science: Paleontology— the study of past geological periods from their fossils

Constellation Find

1. **And**romeda
2. **Boo**tes
3. Camelo**pard**alis
4. **Can**cer
5. **Capri**corn
6. **Car**ina
7. **Cham**aeleon
8. **Crat**er
9. **Gem**ini
10. **Men**sa
11. Micros**cop**ium
12. **Octan**s
13. Pega**sus**
14. **Pho**enix
15. **Sag**ittarius
16. Ser**pens**

Seeing Stars

```
            A R G O
A R I E S
        C E T U S
        D O R A D O
D R A C O
        I N D U S
      L E O
          M U S C A
P I S C E S
  S C O R P I O
```

Answer: A stronomer

123

Opposite Distraction

1. Arm**strong**
2. Dar**win**
3. **Far**aday
4. **Hall**ey
5. **Her**schel
6. **Low**ell
7. Max**well**
8. **Mend**el
9. **New**ton
10. **Past**eur
11. **Dewar**
12. **Wright**

Mini Fill-Ins #2

Fowl

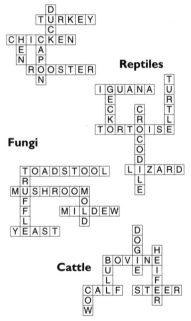

Reptiles

Fungi

Cattle

Leather/Middles Weather Riddles

1. What did the dirt say when it rained? If this keeps up, my name is mud.
2. What do you call it when it rains chickens and ducks? Fowl weather.
3. What did the north wind say to the south wind at the start of the race? On your mark, get set, blow!

4. What did one rain drop say to the other rain drop? My plop is bigger than your plop.
5. What kind of storms do smart kids like? Brain storms.

Simile Scramble

1. Happy as a lark
2. Mad as a hornet
3. Blind as a bat
4. Hungry as a bear
5. Sly as a fox
6. Red as a lobster
7. Loose as a goose
8. Eager as a beaver
9. Slow as a snail
10. Gentle as a lamb
11. Bold as a lion
12. Crazy as a loon
13. Wise as an owl
14. Proud as a peacock
15. Quiet as a mouse
16. Fat as a pig
17. Bald as an eagle
18. Stubborn as a mule
19. Weak as a kitten
20. Busy as a bee

Astronaut's Hangout

AS **T** EROID
BLACK **H** OLE
N **E** BULA

UNIVER **S** E
P LANET
GAL **A** XY
C OMET
MET **E** ORITE

OR **B** IT
S **A** TELLITE
C **R** ATER

Answer: The space bar

Cute Critter

A water bear is a tiny creature no bigger than one grain of sand. When it cannot find water it stops eating, moving, and breathing, and seems to be dead. But when scientists add water to it, the tiny animal comes back to life.

Creature Words

1. Top	10. Tie
2. Bag	11. West
3. Boat	12. Maze
4. Cot	13. Grill
5. Lean	14. Son
6. Lead	15. Feet
7. Hate	16. Crib
8. Jar	17. Rider
9. Sun	18. Dark

Scientist's Snack

F udge
Cook **i** e
Pa **s** try **C** ake
S herbet Doug **h** nut
Brown **i** e **L** i corice
Po **o** pcorn **P** retzel
Ca **n** dy Bi **s** cuit

Riddle answer: Fission chips

Bug Off!

Riddle answer: He is bright for his age.

Creature Body Parts

1. Locust / stomach
2. Jaguar / arms
3. Giraffe / feet
4. Crab / abdomen
5. Turkey / eyebrow
6. Whale / legs
7. Swan / ankle
8. Sardine / neck
9. Finch / chin
10. Wasp / spine
11. Iguana / navel
12. Moth / thigh
13. Mosquito / toes
14. Termite / teeth
15. Toad / adenoids

Cold Stuff

1. Ice	5. Floes
1. Freezer	6. South Pole
2. Penguins	7. Whales
3. Glacier	7. Krill
3. Snow	8. Crevasses
4. Alaska	9. Satellites
4. Alps	10. Blue
5. Seals	10. Blubber

Answer: Continent of Antarctica

Scientific Research #1

1. Bunk	10. Rest
2. Pole	11. Rot
3. Cave	12. Chick
4. Pie	13. Key
5. Doe	14. Chart
6. Fan	15. Bus
7. Gale	
8. Cell	
9. Cure	

Spaced Out

Ear **th**
N **ep** tune
Sp **la** shdown
Engi **ne**
Observa **to** ry
Li **ft** off
Launc **he** r
De **gr** ees
C **ap** sule
R **es** earch

Answer: The planet of the grapes

Scientific Research #2

1. Brain
2. Spy
3. Hare
4. Cost
5. Hue
6. Lake
7. Pain
8. Chin
9. Man
10. Tea
11. Corn
12. Lie
13. Eel
14. Ten
15. Lawn
16. Gas

Museum Guide

1. Califor**nia**
2. **Ma**rine
3. Visi**tor**s
4. **Beach**es
5. **Twenty**-six
6. **Bottle**nose
7. Inverte**brate**s
8. **Can**yon
9. Aba**lone**
10. Urchi**ns**
11. **Weasel**s
12. Al**most**
13. T**ra**ppers
14. En**danger**ed
15. **Along**
16. **Scoop**
17. Cormor**ant**
18. **Mat**erials
19. **Colon**ies
20. **Scav**engers
21. Land**fills**
22. **Jelly**fish
23. Plank**ton**
24. Preser**ved**
25. **Won**derful

Lost Letters

```
S P E A S A N T S T R S T
U R E W O P L C N G C T H
R B R K L D R E S S O S G
G P E B E L S S P H M A I
E N M N Z S E N O H P F F
O G I Q B T Z I T X E A L
N M T R E A D I N G T U I
M A Z E W L C M M H E L N
B R I D E E O O E V Q T G
T H I R T Y P R N T Z Y R
L T U O R T E V C L A P S
N M Y B W X S M O R A L Z
```

1. Stale	B			20. Timer	B	
2. Bacon	E			21. Reading	Y	
3. Faulty	C			22. Power	D	
4. Border	A			23. Copes	I	
5. Dress	U			24. Sole	V	
6. Thirty	S			25. Wring	I	
7. Father	E			26. Mined	D	
8. Surgeon	T			27. Phones	I	
9. Peasant	H			28. Metal	N	
10. Fasts	E			29. Bride	G	
11. Trout	Y					
12. Claps	M			Riddle answer:		
13. Spot	U			Because they		
14. Compete	L			multiply by		
15. Moral	T			dividing		
16. Maze	I					
17. Insect	P					
18. Fight	L					
19. Fling	Y					

Mini Fill-Ins #1

Elements

```
      A       T
    A R S E N I C
O     G       N
X E N O N
Y     N
G   Z
H E L I U M
N
    C E S I U M
```

National Parks

```
        O           Y
      Y E L L O W S T O N E
        Y           S
        M           E
        P       A   M
        I       C   Z I O N
        C       A   T
                A R C H E S
                D
    H A L E A K A L A
```

Water Places

```
    R
A Q U E D U C T   S
    S             T
    E             R
  T R E N C H     A
    V       A     I
    O     I N L E T
    I       A
F J O R D   L
```

Dangerous Sea Critters

```
            C
            O
  B A R R A C U D A
  N       A
  E       L     S Q U I D
  M             H
  O     M O R A Y E E L
  N             R
  S E A S N A K E
```

Uh-Oh!

tor **n** ado   **d** eluge
blizz **a** rd   wh **i** rlwind
winds **t** orm   twi **s** ter
h **u** rricane   squa **l** l
ea **r** thquake   tempe **s** t
g **a** le   **t** yphoon
f **l** ood   cyclon **e**
    r iptide
    land **s** lide

Answer: Natural disasters

Index